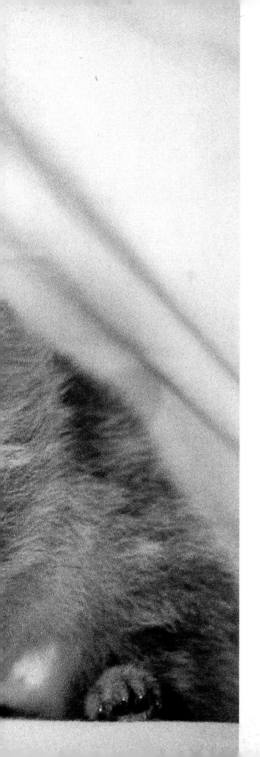

Joe Stahlkuppe

Pomeranians

Everything About
Purchase, Care, Nutrition, Breeding,
Behavior, and Training

Filled with Full-color Photographs

Illustrations by
Michele Earle-Bridges

BARRON'S

CONTENTS

2

UNDERSTANDING THE POMERANIAN

Origin and History

It is ironic that such an open and clearly people-oriented little dog should have a history so shrouded by time and a lack of actual information. But such is the case with the Pomeranian, which takes its name from vague references to the old German province of Pomerania. It was in this Baltic-bordering and obscure region that early specimens of little spitz dogs were purported to originate.

Once thought a part of the Pomeranian origin-mystery, artifacts recovered from excavations in Greece—and other exotic, nonEuropean locations—depicting Pomlike dogs have largely been discounted as having any direct bearing on the breed. The German and European spitz dogs have far too much genetic similarity to the Pomeranian to be only partial ancestors. Pomeranians may not have come exclusively from Pomerania, but northern Europe can claim this breed as its own.

The Pomeranian owes its genetic makeup to that diverse group of sledding, hunting, and herding dogs that sprang from northern Europe, commonly lumped together as the spitz. Its relatives, the Samoyed, the Norwegian

This little Pom is descended from brave sled dogs of the Northland and he seems to know it.

Elkhound, and a number of other northern breeds certainly have proven their worth as workers, companions, and pets. Even the Pomeranian's "big brother"—the Keeshond—once bearing the none-too-flattering name of "the overweight Pomeranian" by early English dog breeders—fits neatly into the worker-companion-pet spitz category.

Stemming from trusted working stock, another Pomeranian irony is that the Pom, as we know it today, is largely a British re-creation complete with ties to the royal family. Queen Victoria, having been exposed to the charm of the larger spitz dogs by her German grandmother, Queen Charlotte, returned from Italy in 1888 with Marco, a smallish spitzlike dog that had become a favorite of hers. So captivated was Victoria that she began breeding and exhibiting specimens of what had come to be called Pomeranians. Her dogs were smaller than the sturdy, 30-pounders of the time, which more closely resembled today's German spitz and American Eskimo dogs than the modern Poms. As a result of her interest in the breed, changes took place that would forever restructure the Pomeranian. The 30-pound (13.6 kg) spitz dog of Queen Victoria's grandmother began its transformation into the lighter Pomeranian, sometimes weighing only about one tenth as much.

The dog-loving public in England, and later in the United States, which had taken the name of a remote German province and shortened it into the fashionable Pom nickname, proceeded to do essentially the same thing with the breed itself. Without losing the jaunty spitz dog confidence and charisma, English dog breeders concentrated on the smallness craze and "breed 'em down in size" became the fancier's credo.

As with most fads, saner heads—and genetic practicality—finally prevailed and the Pomeranian size slide halted at about 5 pounds (2.3 kg) for a number of years. De-emphasizing diminutive size gave these early breeders the opportunity to develop other characteristics, such as

improved coat quality, type, and symmetry. The German spitz dog thus became the raw ore from which the skillful British dog breeders shaped the Pomeranian. It was the English product that was exported to the United States in 1892 where the sprightly little breed soon developed, and has since maintained, a strong, dedicated following.

Unlike other breeds where exaggeration of some particular facet of the breed's makeup, as is true with the decreasing Pom size, would allow unwanted temperament or hidden structural flaws to take root, the Pomeranian attracted friends not only to its tiny size and inborn sense of style, but also to its stable, companionable behavior. British dog fanciers had created a beautiful miniature without sacrificing the attributes that had made the Pom's ancestors valuable workers in a much harsher environment. This exceptional product mixture of attractiveness, alertness, and adaptability combined in this little, big dog to make the Pomeranian a winner—wherever it went.

Nature of the Pom

Whereas the Pomeranian may attract attention because of its appearance, it turns onlookers into admirers and admirers into Pom owners because of its unique personality and an almost eerie ability to relate to its human beings. The latter quality is carried over from its ancestors' long association with humans and remains not only much intact in the modern Pomeranian, but also close to the surface. The camaraderie with humans is one of the many

The Pomeranian has a mischievous but loving personality.

A properly bred and groomed Pomeranian is one of the most beautiful dogs in the world.

reasons that Pom people tend to remain Pom people. Although Pomeranian owners readily admit that they may admire other dog breeds, they tend to agree that the Pomeranian has something special. Most fanciers of this mighty mite back up their feelings with strong breed loyalty. Many cannot even envision their lives without a Pom in there somewhere.

Pomeranians are very bright, both in intelligence and in personality. As such, they need consistent human care and interaction to ensure that these quick-minded little dogs pick up the right habits and the correct behaviors. Usually quite easy to housebreak, Poms have an almost catlike cleanliness. Their keen alertness makes them reasonably easy to train. In fact, some Pomeranians do well in the Obedience ring, where their saucy style and happy nature garner them many fans from among the ringside audience.

Whether achieving in formal Obedience work or not, the well-trained and well-socialized Pomeranian is an excellent companion dog. Its alertness and brave little heart make the Pom a fine early-warning watchdog quite capable of raising a bristling and outraged alarm at the first sign of an intruder. Appropriate training and encouragement will show a young Pom the difference between a legitimate cause for a barking warning and the ordinary "things that go bump in the night" but that pose no danger to the dog or to its household.

Some dog breeders assert that the Pomeranian has canine insight into the moods and feelings of its owner. This apparent empathy causes Pom owners to cite instances in which their pets have picked up on subtle cues in a room or in a situation and acted in an appropriate matter. One owner, long accustomed to the same routine after work each night, found that his female Pomeranian also knew the schedule and would let out a bark if the owner strayed too far off the established time line. This behavior gives new meaning to the term "watchdog."

Characteristic Behavior

Pomeranians quickly put to rest any thought that they are merely animated stuffed animals totally dependent on their owners in every aspect of life. Pomeranians are pert, alert, independent little dogs that possess clearly defined personalities that often seem to hark back to their northern dog ancestry. Poms behave much light their larger counterparts do, and often in an extremely independent fashion.

Pomeranians have a strong sense of personal property and enjoy their own special place or den within the home. This tendency greatly eases crate training and housebreaking. Poms also take much pride in ownership of their belongings—toys, food and water dishes, and other items possessing a value known only to the dog. Although they are not quarrelsome in multidog households, Pomeranians do seem to want to make sure that their unique role in the home and their personal items are left undisturbed.

Sled Dog Behavior

Pom owners have noted marked fastidious eating habits on the part of their dogs. One longtime Pom fan stated that every Pomeranian he had ever owned would always take small bites of food from the food bowl, retreat a certain distance away, and enjoy the morsels at leisure. This interesting behavior may be yet another throwback to the northern dog heritage of the Pomeranian. Noted author Jack London describes just such

Pomeranians are real, living dogs and shouldn't be considered as animated stuffed toys.

Poms are playful and encourage their owners to be playful too.

behavior in some of his discussions of sled dogs, especially in the classic *The Call of the Wild*. Of further interest is the fact that one of the key canine characters in the story was a sled dog called Spitz, a name still associated with the not-too-distant history of the Pomeranian.

Another possible carryover from sled dog origins may be the evident love that most Poms seem to have for traveling. Especially when proper safeguards are taken, the Pomeranian makes an excellent pet for those who like to be accompanied by their dog on short trips or even on more extended vacations. The Pomeranian is small, clean, interested in its surroundings, and adaptable—all good tourist attributes.

Kinship with Humans

The Pomeranian possesses a keenness of mind and a sweetness of spirit that has endeared the breed to millions of people the world over. Its behavior seems consistent with its reputation as a superb companion dog. The Pomeranian is seemingly endowed with a sense of propriety, and its behavior rarely is out of step with the situation. Poms are fun-loving dogs when fun is the order of the day and yet they can be more sedate when events demand calmer or quieter actions. Owners of Pomeranians who have suffered a family death or some other loss have reported clearly sympathetic behavior from their dogs when sadness has been evident.

This red Pom and its cream pal get along well together. Pomeranians are gregarious toward other dogs and people.

Even Pom puppies seem to show this tendency. One owner reported an extremely reserved atmosphere surrounding a litter on the day one puppy had left for a new home.

An unusual story of one Pomeranian owner illustrates the breed's kinship with human attitudes. A young Pom was owned by an elderly person who suddenly became gravely ill. Very little hope was held out for recovery and family members were summoned to the sick person's home. Throughout the ordeal, the normally lively Pomeranian had been very staid and reserved, but at some point its behavior changed. The little dog began to bark and run excitedly around the floor near the sickbed. The dog's owner opened his eyes and smiled at the little dog—the first sign of recovery that brought the owner several more years of relatively good health and definitely good companionship from his Pom. Family members believe the little dog actually sensed the improvement in his owner and reacted to it.

Intelligence, Energy, and Loyalty

The Pomeranian is brave, but rarely foolhardy. It will bristle and make its presence known to strangers or potential enemies. The Pom's actions are such that it stays just out of harm's way while actively making its displeasure abundantly and vocally clear. Normally a friendly and happy dog, the Pomeranian will make friends on its own terms and only after it is sure of one's intentions. Because of its intelligence and its high activity level, the Pomeranian needs to have its brightness and energy channeled into appropriate behaviors. With some simple, consistent training, the Pom can become an excellent watchdog, discerning unusual sounds from the ordinary. The genetic capacity that has made the Pomeranian a good Obedience trial dog also makes it a faithful protector of its domain.

No dog is more devoted to its owner than the Pomeranian. The breed's adaptability allows the Pom to fit into life in an apartment, a suburban duplex, or a rural home. Although constraints *must* be placed on very young children—as they must with any of the toy breeds—the Pomeranian can become an excellent child's pet as well as an incomparable companion for an older person. Given the almost uncanny ability of these little dogs to pick up on certain cues and learn quickly what is expected of them, there are few breeds that can boast an overall better record of satisfied owners than the Pomeranian. As has been mentioned, this loyalty is amply demonstrated by the number of people who, after having owned a Pom, stay with the breed—enthusiastically.

Vocal Expression

Pomeranians are vocal little dogs. Their basic alertness makes them prone to barking if something seems amiss, but it is important that Poms be given adequate training to help them avoid becoming nuisance barkers. Whereas one Pomeranian may be a "yapper" and the next Pom may bark only when it is appropriate to do so, consistent training is *always* a valuable aid. A lack of training is generally the reason for most of the Poms that have been classified as noisy, as is probably the case with noisy dogs of any breed.

Longtime breeders have numerous stories of their Poms seeming to be attempting some form of vocal communication with their owners. The earlier reference made to the Pom owner whose little female kept him on schedule may be an example of just such behavior.

Pomeranians, especially puppies, are often very frail and could be easily injured or killed.

When this man arrived home each evening, he would go through a set of routine activities—removing his work clothes, showering, eating dinner—before he could relax and spend time with his dog. She would follow his progress through each activity. If he spent a little too much time in the shower, or lingered too long over dessert, the Pom would begin to make muttering noises that would end with a sharp yelp, reminding him to get a move on. Her owner could clearly differentiate between her monitoring behavior and a bark to alert him to some outside noise.

Adaptability

One of the strongest attributes of the Pomeranian is its ability to fit into its environment. To this end, it amply uses its mental and physical capacities. Breeders and owners like to point out how well the Pom does in Obedience work, in the show ring, as a companion dog, as a therapy dog, and as an alert home watchdog. Not surprisingly, these people are convinced about the Pom. It is therefore interesting to note how many *non*-Pomeranian owners have recognized the adaptability of the Pom. Veterinarians, dog groomers, dog show officials, and others who are outside Pomeranian circles are often strong in their praise of the breed, claiming almost as many superlatives for Pomeranians as do the

This red Pomeranian strikes a pose worthy of its larger ancestors.

Pom people themselves. Few people who really get to know Poms have other than positive feelings about them. This speaks well for the image that the little dogs have established on trips outside their homes. Some of the staunchest supporters of the breed—other than breeders and owners, of course—are those who have seen Poms in a different light from that of their owners. Even casual observers, who would be the most likely objective viewers of any breed, have a high positivity quotient about Pomeranians.

This adaptability of the Pomeranian was one of the reasons that British royalty was initially attracted to the little spitz dogs. That same adaptability remains one of the great strengths of the breed today and one of the key reasons for the widespread acceptance of the Pomeranian.

Mental Ability

Although the physical attractiveness of the Pomeranian, especially of puppies and show dogs, could account for a certain portion of the breed's great popularity, appearance is certainly not the sole reason. Cuteness and overall beauty will go only so far in assuring owner loyalty, either to an individual dog or to a specific breed.

The number of Poms in the Obedience ring speaks volumes about the way owners view the mental capacities of their little dogs. Success in this endeavor also strengthens the public perception of the Pom's intelligence and trainability. Obedience work, done in strict accordance with stringent rules and procedures, is also under the ever-watchful eye of the ringside crowd. An opportunity to shine can quickly turn into a chance to do poorly—all right out there in public. That Poms and their owners are willing and able to sustain themselves and even thrive in this environment gives good evidence of the smarts of the breed.

Less formal and less structured proof comes from Pomeranian owners and breeders. *Every* Pom owner seems to have an entire collection of stories illustrating great Pom mental acuity.

Some Poms don't realize they are not as big as other dogs. Pomeranian owners need to be careful that a little dog with big courage doesn't get hurt.

Another of the reasons cited by Queen Victoria for her attraction to and championing of the breed was its intelligence.

The mental ability of Pomeranians has made the breed more than just another lapdog kept exclusively for its unique appearance and many pet qualities. Pomeranians have always been excellent companion animals, but one Pomeranian did more than fill his owner's life with companionship; this Pomeranian was credited with saving his owner's life. Undeterred by the smoke, the flames, and the general panic that house fires usually produce, a Pomeranian, by "barking and running in front," led a firefighter through a smoke-filled home to his unconscious owner. The dog reportedly barked long enough and loud enough to get the attention of the firefighter and the dog's owner was rescued. Although he spent several

days in critical condition in a hospital intensive care unit, this Pom owner lived to go home to his family and to the dog that saved his life.

Pomeranians are very smart and as such bring a special responsibility to their owners or would-be owners. In order for this little dog to become the super pet, Obedience dog, show dog, or all-around companion that it can be, the Pom will need consistent treatment and adequate training.

Body Language

You have only to see a Pomeranian "strut its stuff" down an aisle at a dog show or "do its thing" in an Obedience or Agility event, to know that this tiny dog has a definite physical

This beautiful Pom face amply illustrates the perky brightness that accounts for a large part of this breed's popularity.

presence that almost magnetically draws the attention of onlookers. Pom owners claim that many Pomeranians rise to such occasions and actually show great enjoyment in being in the public eye.

Pomeranians, although not normally hostile to other dogs, are not passive whiners either. When encountering a larger dog, the Pom may often bristle up its stiff and considerable coat, as if to make itself appear as large as possible. The Pomeranian will stand its ground, but it will not normally seek a conflict if other options, such as an alert owner, are available.

This behavior again seems to stem from actions commonly observed in other members of the extended spitz family of breeds. Initially, while in usually rough conditions, these Pomeranian ancestors were worker-sled dogs, and indiscriminate battling was absolutely not to be tolerated. Dogs were valuable workers and fighting wasted both time and dogs. The Pom may have gained its "discretion is the better part of valor" approach from this ancestral source.

Strangers

Human strangers often get much the same reception from the Pomeranian. The Pom will vocally make its presence known, remaining a safe distance away, clearly analyzing the human being as to intent. As mentioned, the Pom remembers its friends and its foes. This memory makes early and consistent socialization and training of puppies all the more essential. A lack of awareness by someone with such a percep-tive little dog can lead to lingering misunderstandings. Whereas some breeds will accept almost any person as an immediate friend, the Pom is a bit more reticent and cautious. This is clearly illustrated in the Pom's body language.

When confronted with a new person, the Pom often will dance away from early attempts by a stranger to pet it or to pick it up. This is seen in even very young puppies that will stay coyly just out of reach until, almost as if by some secret signal, acceptance is bestowed upon the human. The boundaries and "no man's land" imposed by the Pom become decreasingly small until the friendly dog or puppy is within easy grasp. The Pomeranian loves attention and petting, but by this "come hither, go yonder" routine makes it clear that any interaction will be strictly on the dog's terms.

The Sensory Organs

As one might suspect with any breed as keen and bright as the Pomeranian, the breed possesses exceptional sensory abilities. The terms *alert* and *foxlike* have been used aptly to describe the Pom. These terms scarcely could apply to a sluggish, inactive dog or to a member of a breed that fashion had left less than ready to face the world by adding flop ears or heavy bangs or other sensory-undermining characteristics. Sharp eyes, excellent hearing, and a surprising acuity in sense of smell have made the Pom the alert little dog that it is.

Eyes and Ears

The large, expressive eyes of the Pomeranian are among the first physical aspects that one notices about the breed. Large eyes enable the Pom to survey its domain and be instantly aware of things in its surroundings. Good eyesight is

certainly one of the reasons for the Pomeranian's general success in the Obedience ring. This intelligent little dog doesn't miss much.

The ears of the Pomeranian remain much like those of its sled dog ancestors, attractive yet utilitarian. They have not been tampered with by breeders striving to make a particular genetic fashion statement. They require no surgery or inordinate molding to make them presentable. Again, breeders are full of accounts about how Pomeranians are able to differentiate between similar sounds—the step of its owner on the stairs as opposed to that of a stranger, or the sound of its owner's car door from the sound of all other car doors. One Pomeranian had the ability to listen to the cues her owner gave during telephone conversations to indicate when the conversation might be coming to an end. The Pom had been taught not to bark or bother her owner while the owner was on the phone. This dog became quite skillful in picking up phrases or even rises of inflection that signaled the end of the conversation. She would remain perfectly quiet throughout the call but, upon hearing such indicators, would let out a bark of relief often before the receiver had left the owner's ear.

In some pet breeds, natural abilities seem to have been decimated; not so with the Pomeranian. It appears to have eyesight and hearing equal to the best of its larger spitz family relatives, including those still actively used in sled dog and other work.

Smell and Taste

One breeder gives a remarkable account concerning the scenting ability of one Pom puppy. This breeder had received a pick-of-the-litter puppy in lieu of a stud fee. Only a few minutes after the puppy's arrival, the breeder's young child was playing with him in the driveway of their home. Some other children from the neighborhood came by and invited the child to come with them to play ball. The child put the Pom pup back into the traveling crate in which he had arrived, and went off to play with friends. He failed to adequately latch the crate and the pup got out and trailed his new friend nearly one-half mile. Within a few minutes, the breeder's child was astonished to see the new puppy at the ball field.

The sense of smell is another area where the Pomeranian seems to have lost none of its ancestral abilities. Scenting ability in the Pom, according to experienced dog people, seems to be on a par with its excellent eyesight and acute hearing.

Pomeranians have a reputation for being somewhat careful eaters. They seem to relish the taste of good-quality food while clearly rejecting more mundane fare. It would be unfair to call them picky about their food, but Poms do have definite likes and dislikes. (Feeding will be discussed in more detail in the chapter beginning on page 41, but this does appear to be another area where early training can get the Pom off to a good start.) A dog of any breed can be spoiled by inappropriate feeding practices that can lead to poor eating habits. With a dog as smart as the Pom, care must be taken to feed it quality food from the beginning and to make any dietetic changes gradually and only when necessary.

Touch

Although Poms may be somewhat reserved and guarded with strangers, once that stranger is acknowledged as a friend, the Pomeranian greatly enjoys physical contact, seeming to actually luxuriate in the touch of a favored human. This makes veterinary care easier with Pomeranians than with some breeds that seem to resent the human touch, especially from a human other than their owners. Some veterinarians assert that once a Pom knows and trusts a veterinarian, the dog often seems to readily accept the entire experience.

A note of caution: The Pomeranian is a dog of acute sensibilities; this is also true of its sense of touch. Corporal punishment may be felt by a Pom much more sharply than needed or intended, especially by a young dog. It is important to note that the Pomeranian can be negatively affected by overly physical reprimanding. Small children or unthinking or inexperienced adults can do real damage, both physically and mentally, by striking a Pomeranian. *Don't hit any pets, but especially not a Pom!*

Meeting Other Dogs

As mentioned earlier, the Pomeranian is a brave and intelligent little dog. The accent here must certainly emphasize *little*. Whereas the Pom certainly is not foolhardy in attacking larger dogs, it is still a dog and, as a dog, may decide that an attack is warranted. It is crucial that a little dog's owner recognize the danger if such a confrontation were to take place. As with small children and Pomeranians, a larger, stronger dog, perhaps not even meaning any damage, can seriously injure a 5- or 6-pound (2.3–2.7-kg) Pom. All reasonable care must be taken to lessen the chances of this occurring.

Under normal circumstances, the Pomeranian can meet and interact with other dogs without much potential jeopardy. There are always situations, however, and the Pom may not

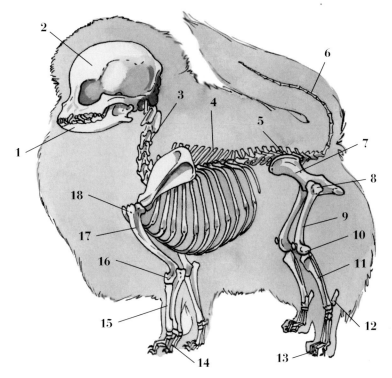

The skeletal system
of a Pomeranian.
1. lower jaw (mandible)
2. skull (cranium)
3. cervical vertebrae
4. thoracic vertebrae
5. lumbar vertebrae
6. tail vertebrae
7. pelvis
8. hip joint
9. femur
10. knee joint (stifle)
11. tibia and fibula
12. hock (tarsas)
13. metatarsals
14. metacarpals
15. radius and ulna
16. elbow
17. humerus
18. shoulder joint

always be able to skitter away from trouble. The bristling confidence of the Pom may be enough to discourage hostility in a well-behaved larger dog. Nevertheless, not every larger dog that a Pom can possibly encounter will be well behaved. With dogs of its own relative size, the Pomeranian is quite capable of maintaining its own sense of decorum. It is interesting to note that Poms in a multidog, multibreed household generally serve as peacemakers rather than instigators. Several Pomeranians in a home quickly work out their own accommodations and arrangements with sled dog-like efficiency and effectiveness.

AKC Standard

General Appearance: The Pomeranian is a compact, short-backed, active toy dog. He has a soft, dense undercoat with a profuse harsh-textured outer coat. His heavily plumed tail is set high and lies flat on his back. He is alert in character, exhibits intelligence in expression, is buoyant in deportment, and is inquisitive by nature. The Pomeranian is cocky, commanding, and animated as he gaits. He is sound in composition and action.

Size, Proportion, Substance: The average weight of the Pomeranian is from three to seven pounds, with the ideal weight for the

Underneath the impressive Pomeranian coat is a short-bodied but muscular little dog. The muscle structure of the Pom clearly reveals the miniature sled dog physique.

show specimen being four to six pounds. Any dog over or under the limits is objectionable. However, overall quality is to be favored over size. The distance from the point of shoulder to the point of buttocks is slightly shorter than from the highest point of the withers to the ground, the distance from the brisket to the ground is half the height at the withers. He is medium-boned, and the length of his legs is in proportion to a well-balanced frame. When examined, he feels sturdy.

Head: The *head* is in balance with the body. The *muzzle* is rather short, straight, fine, free of lippiness and never snipey. His *expression* is alert and may be referred to as fox-like. The *skull* is closed. The top of the skull is slightly rounded, but not domed. When viewed from the front and side, one sees small *ears* which

are mounted high and carried erect. To form a wedge, visualize a line from the tip of the nose ascending through the center of the eyes and the tip of the ears. The *eyes* are dark, bright, medium in size and almond-shaped. They are set well into the skull on either side of a well-pronounced stop. The pigment is black on the nose and eye rims except self-colored in brown, beaver, and blue dogs. The *teeth* meet in a scissors bite. One tooth out of alignment is acceptable. *Major Faults:* Round, domed skull; undershot mouth; overshot mouth.

Neck, Topline, Body: The *neck* is short with its base set well into the shoulders to allow the head to be carried high. The *back* is short with a level *topline*. The *body* is compact and well-ribbed with brisket reaching the elbow. The plumed *tail* is one of the characteristics of the breed, and lies flat and straight on the back.

Forequarters: The Pomeranian has sufficient layback of shoulders to carry the neck and head proud and high. The *shoulders* are moderately muscled. The length of the shoulder blade and upper arm are equal. The *forelegs* are straight and parallel to each other. Height from elbows to withers approximately equals height from ground to elbow. The pasterns are straight and strong. The *feet* are well-arched, compact, and turn neither in nor out. He stands well up on his toes. *Dewclaws* may be removed. *Major Faults:* Down in pasterns.

Hindquarters: The angulation of the hindquarters balances that of the forequarters. The buttocks are well behind the set of the tail. The thighs are moderately muscled with *stifles* that are moderately bent and clearly defined. The hocks are perpendicular to the ground and the *legs* are straight and parallel to each other. The *feet* are well-arched, compact, and turn neither in nor out. He stands well up on his toes. *Dewclaws,* if any on the hind legs, may be removed. *Major Faults:* Cowhocks or lack of soundness in hind legs or stifles.

Gait: The Pomeranian's gait is smooth, free, balanced and vigorous. He has good reach in his forequarters and strong drive with his hindquarters. Each rear leg moves in line with the foreleg on the same side. To achieve balance, his legs converge slightly inward toward a center line beneath his body. The rear and front legs are thrown neither in nor out. The topline remains level, and his overall balance is maintained.

Coat: A Pomeranian is noted for its double coat. The *undercoat* is soft and dense. The *outercoat* is long, straight, glistening and harsh in texture. A thick undercoat will hold up and permit the guard hair to stand off from the Pomeranian's body. The coat is abundant from the neck and fore part of the shoulders and chest, forming a frill which extends over the shoulders and chest. The head and leg coat is tightly packed and shorter in length than that of the body. The forequarters are well-feathered to the hock. The tail is profusely covered with long, harsh, spreading straight hair. Trimming for neatness and a clean outline is permissible. *Major Faults:* Soft, flat or open coat.

Color: All colors, patterns and variations thereof are allowed and must be judged on an equal basis. *Patterns: Black and Tan*—tan or rust sharply defined, appearing above each eye and on muzzle, throat, and forechest, on all legs and feet and below the tail. The richer the tan the more desirable; *Brindle*—the base color is gold, red, or orange-brindled with strong black cross stripes; *Parti-color*—is white with any other color distributed in patches with a white blaze preferred on the head. *Classifications:* The Open Classes at specialty shows may be divided by color as follows: Open Red, Orange, Cream, and Sable; Open Black, Brown, and Blue; Open Any Other Color, Pattern, or Variation.

Temperament: The Pomeranian is an extrovert, exhibiting great intelligence and a vivacious spirit, making him a great companion dog as well as a competitive show dog. *Even though a toy dog, the Pomeranian must be subject to the same requirements of soundness and structure prescribed for all breeds, and any deviation from the ideal described in the standard should be penalized to the extent of the deviation.*

Approved December 9, 1996
Effective January 31, 1997

CONSIDERATIONS BEFORE YOU BUY

Are You Ready?

Here are some basic questions that you should candidly answer before you go a step further toward Pom ownership. If a Pomeranian is to be a sometime pet, a fashion accessory, or something to make you look cool, forget about it! If you want a perpetual puppy that will always be a cute and tiny munchkin of about eight weeks old, grow up yourself. If you want a canine companion that never sheds, never leaves a puddle or a pile in an inappropriate place, clean up your thinking and get a virtual pet on your computer.

Pomeranians are living, breathing, loving pets that will have all the bodily functions of most other dogs, will go through the same age phases that other dogs do, and on anyone's absolute perfection meter will fail to reach 100 percent, as with all other pets—and people. A realistic look at your lifestyle, your expectations, and yourself is essential *before* you bring a Pomeranian into your home. Realistically gauge yourself on these questions and you'll have a better vision about owning a Pom.

✔ Does *each* person in your home know and understand what having a Pom will mean and entail?

The Pomeranian beauty, charm, and ability are all there. The right owner will bring it all out.

✔ Does *each* person in your home willingly accept this role and its responsibilities?

✔ Is each person enthusiastic about sharing time and attention with a new pet?

✔ Does your family, as a group, have enough quality time to bring in a new family member?

✔ Does your family have the financial resources to undertake a long-term relationship with a pet that will rely on you totally?

✔ Does your family have the maturity and emotional stability if, at first, your Pom barks too much, chews up valuable things, and causes messes on carpets and floors?

✔ Do you and your family want a commitment that brings an emotional price tag if your new pet should become injured, ill, or even die?

✔ Is your family willing to enlist others, such as veterinarians, trainers, and Pom breeders, to solve problems that may confront your pet?

✔ Is your family more interested in owning a dog than gaining a new, and admittedly furry, new family member?

When answering these questions, remember that for you, a failure will mean returning a dog to its breeder, finding your dog a new home, or even taking this Pom to the animal shelter. For the Pomeranian you thought you wanted, leaving you will mean being rejected by the humans it has come to worship and adore. Even if Pomeranians—or just this particular Pom—don't fit in with your family, this pet now faces an unhappy and uncertain future. Helping you to avoid this—for you and the Pomeranian—is reason enough for these personal questions. Do yourself and your potential Pomeranian pet a big favor, and answer them as honestly as possible.

Puppy or Adult?

Part of the answer to the age of the Pom you obtain hinges on what end purpose you have in mind for the dog. Obedience work, Agility, or a dog show career can usually be best accomplished by purchasing a pup from appropriate breeding stock and working with that pup as it grows up. As companions, there may very well be adult Pomeranians available. You can check with local Pom breeders or with the American Pomeranian Club (see page 92 for address).

Bringing a puppy into your home is much like bringing a human baby into your home. This is a totally dependent entity that will need much care, love, and supervision. Like a human

baby, a Pom baby will make messes, cry in the middle of the night, and require a lot of attention. A Pom baby will need to be handled gently and given the first, rudimentary steps in becoming a well-trained adult Pom.

Some responsible person should help the Pom puppy adjust to its new home. This will require time and effort. Be certain that this person wants to do this crucial job and is able to successfully do it.

A puppy will need consistent care, without fail, as a high priority. Perhaps the cavalryman in the Old West, who could not eat or rest until he had taken care of his horse, sets a good example for model dog owners. A puppy or an older dog should receive attention before any other activity. You brought it here; it didn't come uninvited.

An older Pomeranian may not need as much immediate attention or supervision as a puppy, but even a well-trained adult dog will need some adjustment time in its new home. An older dog may even have a particular set of problem dynamics. It may have been mistreated and, as a result, be snappish and defensive. It may have been closely attached to someone in its previous home and may grieve, sometimes even to the point of risking ill health. The adult dog may have learned another lifestyle and have some difficulty adjusting to yours. There are any number of problems that can and do arise, but an aware new Pom owner can find a way to resolve most of them. Remember that Pomeranians are famous for their adaptability.

Pom puppies are adorable and are sometimes purchased on impulse— a bad idea, especially for the puppy.

How a puppy develops will depend largely on how it is chosen and the kind of care it receives.

If you are a first-time dog owner or a new Pom person, perhaps the best route to take would be to start a regimen of study. Books, Pom breeders, veterinarians, and other dog professionals can help you avoid major pitfalls, but only if you will listen and then apply what you have learned.

Male or Female?

Both male and female Pomeranians make wonderful pets and can have sparkling careers in the Obedience or show ring. Females are affectionate, clearly feminine, and often become very attached to their families (as do males). Unless you have serious thoughts about breeding Pomeranians, which will be discussed later (see page 55), then either a male or a female should do equally well.

Spaying and Neutering

If you choose a female and showing is not your goal, have her spayed. All the problems that can stem from your female coming "in season" will be eliminated. However, spaying will keep her from being eligible for entry in a dog show. Males can also be neutered, which will not affect their pet quality and will actually make them more tractable if they should come into contact with unspayed females. Spayed females and neutered males can still compete in many other sanctioned Pom activities. Unless

you have *serious* plans to enter Pom breeding, spaying or neutering your dog is a wise move.

Male Aggression

A male Pom is all male in spite of his small size. He will have a tendency to mark his territory on walks and outings. A male can show some aggressive behavior when confronted with strange dogs, but good training and good supervision on your part can prevent any potentially dangerous confrontations with larger dogs. It is wise to remember that the male Pomeranian may not always realize that he is much smaller than some adversaries. As with small children, larger dogs can do severe damage to a Pomeranian. Even a playful puppy of a larger breed could hurt your Pomeranian. Guard against this by being alert to any situation where such a tragedy could occur.

This pet-quality Pomeranian still thinks it looks pretty good in the mirror.

Note: When bringing a Pom into a home where there is a cat, the same sort of preventive care must be undertaken. Some cats are much larger than any Pomeranian. With its prominent eyes and inquisitive nature, a Pom, especially a youngster, could sustain an eye injury from a well-aimed paw by a disgruntled feline.

Breeding

If breeding Pomeranians seems to be an area of interest to you—but only after a great deal of careful study and consideration—you might well be advised to purchase the best-quality female puppy available. If she happens to do well in the show ring or comes from an exceptional line of dogs that have done well there, you may be able to breed her to a stud dog of good repute and compatible pedigree. It is wise to remember that dog breeding is best accomplished only by serious dog breeders who have the improvement of the breed as their ultimate goal. Just breeding your Pom bitch to have her experience having puppies is an irresponsible attitude for you to take and a wise one to avoid. (For more on breeding, see the chapter that begins on page 55.)

Purchasing a male puppy in hopes that he will become a top-producing stud dog is the longest of long shots. Even for lifetime Pomeranian breeders, to obtain such a male puppy is rare indeed. Owning an unneutered male of lesser quality just on the off-chance that someone would want to breed to him is another irresponsible attitude. To breed specifically for pet quality, when even the very best show matings produce many more pet specimens than show dogs, is always a terrible idea as long as there are so many unwanted puppies born each year that need loving homes.

Pet or Show Quality?

It is important to decide whether you want a pet-quality puppy or a show-quality puppy. "Pet quality" should never be a catchall phrase for reject puppies any more than "show quality" automatically guarantees you a top show dog in the future.

Pet-quality puppies may be excellent Agility, therapy, or Obedience dogs and can excel as companion dogs. As a rule, these pups have some little conformation flaws that make it impossible for them to be considered for the show ring. These flaws are generally cosmetic in form, such as being a little too large, and should not include any physical disabilities or conditions that would make or cause such a puppy to be unhealthy or unsound. As a rule, pet-quality puppies are also not viewed as potential breeding stock.

Show-quality puppies are much harder to locate. Some breeders are reluctant to sell a puppy with show potential to a first-time Pom owner or to an owner who may not be able to allow the puppy to reach its full show potential. Show-quality puppies will be considerably more expensive than pet-quality puppies, but if showing your Pom is your ultimate goal, study hard and buy the best possible puppy from the best possible stock. Occasionally, breeders will make arrangements that will allow a serious dog exhibitor to own a dog in partnership with the breeder. Other similar deals also may exist if you want a breeding dog of sound show stock. These arrangements, while not common, do happen. They usually hinge on whether you possess the

TIP

Male or Female?

Both male and female Pomeranians make excellent pets. The little females possess a sweetness that makes them superior pets for older people. The little males are perky dogs that have won people over who never thought they could admire, much less own, a small dog. The choice of a male or female for you, if you want a good pet, is an easy one. Just pick out the male or female that you like the best! You won't go wrong, either way.

skill and motivation to give a show dog the best possible exposure and on whether you can convince a serious Pom breeder that you do.

Pet-quality puppies, though less expensive and generally more available than show-quality puppies, should be healthy, happy Poms quite capable of becoming a key part of your life. If showing (or breeding) is not in your game plan, a spayed or neutered pet-quality Pomeranian is obviously tailored precisely to your needs.

Selecting a Puppy

Before you begin the selection process, there are a number of things that will make your task easier and less of a gamble.

Pomeranians need good food, housing, grooming, and care to develop their impressive coats.

✔ Read as much as you can about the Pomeranian.
✔ Contact the breed clubs and breeders in the area (see page 92 for addresses).
✔ Visit dog shows and chat with breeder-exhibitors there. Look at their show Poms. See what the breed is supposed to look like at its very best. In short, get to know the Pom before you set out on your quest.
✔ Visually inspect as many Poms as possible and, if you have a color preference, take time

to look at many dogs of the same color; a color preference is probably natural, but if you are looking for a pet and a good one of a different color turns up, don't ignore it.

Show Quality

✔ If you are after a show-quality puppy, stick with quality breeders who may help you find the puppy you are seeking. Forget about bargain basement Poms that may come your way.

✔ Center your thinking not only on one specific Pomeranian, but on a specific family or "line."

✔ Concentrate on the specific attributes you want such a puppy to possess.

✔ Find out which breeder has a top reputation—not just a top show record.

✔ Do a lot of questioning and listening and refrain from buying any puppy unless it fits the precise model you have thoughtfully constructed. Remember, even with the best breeder selling you the puppy of the highest possible potential, not every such situation produces a winning show dog—and winning is the main reason dogs are shown.

To pick a show-quality puppy, you would do well to make friends with a Pom breeder who can help you best apply the written descriptions in the Pomeranian Breed Standard (see pages 17–19) to a young puppy. Finding the show puppy you are seeking may be a long, arduous process, but if showing is a sincere goal, it is the only way you can go about it. While most breeders are honest, helpful people, "buyer beware" is always a good motto when you are new in any interest area, including show dogs.

Pet Quality

Finding a pet-quality puppy may be much simpler, but can be as potentially risky. Just because you are planning to spend hundreds for a pet rather than thousands for a show pup doesn't mean that you should not read, study, compare, check around, and try to find the best-quality puppy. Remember that we are talking about adding a family member that will be with you for perhaps a decade or more. Care is the watchword.

Your search for the right Pom should center on the best sources. Seek out reputable breeders whose reputation is based on the quality of the dogs and puppies they have to sell. Avoid the "fast food" approach to purchasing a pet; haste in buying the first Pomeranian you see may lead you and your family down a very bad and sad path. Impulsively picking a poor-quality Pom now may become a real problem for you down the line. You may have chosen the wrong breed, the wrong dog in the wrong breed, or the wrong dog in the wrong breed from the wrong source. You may be annoyed when a pet doesn't work out—the pet will be devastated. You can always find another dog, but if your unwanted pet bounces from owner to owner or ends up in an animal shelter to face a very uncertain future, it is a very sad situation.

A pet-quality Pomeranian could come from a breeder of show stock. Because many more pet puppies than show pups are produced, you should be able to find a good pup from this source. In this case, you have a chance to look at your pup's environment. Ask to see the parents of the puppy. Most breeders welcome potential puppy buyers who will take the time to check things out. They know these buyers are the ones most likely to give a puppy the care it deserves. Professional dog breeders are concerned about their reputations and are also faced with finding good homes for their excess

TIP

Picking Up a Puppy

If you are visiting several sources looking for a Pom puppy, always wash your hands with antibacterial soap or wipes between stops. It would be tragic to think that you were responsible for transmitting some disease to several litters of Pomeranian puppies.

The best way to handle a tiny Pom puppy is to gently pick it up supporting the back and rear end with one hand and the chest with the other. The puppy will feel supported, more comfortable, and therefore safer.

When lifting a Pomeranian puppy, always place a supporting hand under the hindquarters. Remember to be gentle when handling the tiny youngster.

pet-quality pups. While you are looking for a place from which to obtain a good pet Pom puppy, they are looking for a good owner for one of their not-quite-show specimens. This can, and often does, work out for all three of you—the breeder, you, and the puppy.

Backyard breeders: You may be tempted to seek out the readily available "bargain basement" Pomeranian. If you can't afford to get a good Pom, you can't afford one at all. Classified ads and notes on a sell-and-swap bulletin board may be from conscientious Pom owners who have an extra puppy of good quality. But how will you know? The odds are against an inexperienced backyard breeder being able to sell a puppy of sufficient quality to an inexperienced Pom seeker.

You are definitely on your own when you choose a source that can't give you a real guarantee on the long-term health and temperament of any puppy you may want to buy. If you want a really good pet-quality puppy that can grow into a very good pet, start with top-quality show breeders who are striving for real quality. Their non-show or pet prospects may be more expensive than a Pom from the bulletin board at the corner store or some other bargain source, but you stand an infinitely greater chance of getting what you really want—a good Pomeranian.

Pet Stores

You will probably need a good pet store to serve as a source of many of the things your Pom puppy will need, such as premium food, a large assortment of toys, crates, collars and leads, helpful books, and information. A knowledgeable pet store person can be a very valuable asset to you.

This young lady and her Pomeranian have a lot to offer each other in terms of love and companionship.

Many stores can help put you in touch with high-quality Pom breeders who may have the puppy you are seeking. In any case, having a good, local pet store available for supplies, information, and general advice is always very helpful.

Breeders

"Diamonds in the rough" are tough, if not impossible, to find. Seek a potential show-quality pup from a show-oriented breeder. An Obedience trial puppy probably should come from stock that has distinguished itself in the Obedience ring. Decide what you want in the puppy and then go to the place you are most likely to find it.

To sum up, when choosing a Pom pup, take time to observe the puppies. Don't ruin all the effort you have made up to this point by fixating on one puppy and making your ideal fit that pup because it's there and so are you. Stick with your game plan and make every effort to determine if the puppies shown fit what you are seeking. Remember that you are seeking a sound, healthy puppy that will be a family member/companion for years to come. If you act impulsively now, you may have a lot of time to regret it in the future.

Papers

Prior to actually choosing a puppy from any source, make sure you will receive three things:

1. The puppy's health records, showing dates of vaccination, deworming, and a health certificate, signed by a veterinarian stating that the puppy has been examined and appears healthy.

2. The American Kennel Club (AKC) registration certificate stating that your Pom is a purebred. With this certificate you should also receive application papers to send to the AKC to register the puppy in your name.

3. A pedigree, which is really only as good as the source from which the puppy comes, showing the pup's parents and recent lineage.

These documents are very important and if they are not available, don't buy the puppy.

Making the Selection

Assuming that all the papers are in order and you feel that the source you have chosen will be reliable and will guarantee the puppy to be

This young boy and his young Pom have much to learn, but they can do it.

decide what kind of puppy that is, should be no real problem.

Carefully handle each puppy that fits your requirements, remembering that a six- to eight-week-old puppy will not clearly reflect all that it may become. Depending on the amount of contact with outsiders the puppies have had, they may be somewhat apprehensive at your approach, but you can tell if they seem healthy and you can see if they appear sound and not overly frightened by your visit.

You may not find exactly what you are seeking, but don't be afraid to walk away. There are other puppies, and this is a long-term relationship that you are planning. If that special puppy is there, the one that is bold, bright-eyed, and fits your requirements, you may have found your new family member. The accent is on the word *may*. You want to refrain from mentally and emotionally deciding on the puppy until *your* veterinarian has had a chance to inspect it and pronounce it sound and healthy.

Time taken now will be well worth it later, when this friendly puppy becomes the ideal companion that has been the object of all your reading, questioning, and searching.

Poms and Children

Pomeranians and very small children do not mix. This is not the dog's fault, but merely a realistic assertion that small children can seriously, sometimes even fatally, injure very small dogs. Little legs can easily break with rough treatment and a little dog jumping from a

healthy and sound—it's always best to have this in writing—the time for selection is at hand. You already have an idea of what you want—male or female, color, quality, and so on—and hopefully you have chosen a source that will give you several puppies from which to choose. Pomeranians usually have very small litters—one, two, or maybe three puppies—so you may have to wait to get a puppy that fits color or other specific requirements that you and your family may have. Waiting for exactly the right puppy, after you have taken the time to really child's arms can be all that it would take for the Pom to be hurt. Small children must *always* be supervised when they are playing with a Pomeranian.

Not even all older children are mature enough to be left unsupervised with a fragile Pomeranian puppy—or an adult for that matter. Let common sense guide you in these matters. The safety of your pet should be your prime concern.

Expenses

A pet-quality Pom puppy should cost you about $400; show pups can cost $1,000 or more. A reasonable pet-level budget for veterinary care, premium pet food, and other items should be about $50 per month. Good care will save you additional dollars.

"Teacup" Poms

The so-called "teacup" Pomeranians are a mistake. Don't buy one! These ultratiny Poms of 1 or 2 pounds (0.5–0.9 kg) may be cute, but they are usually a huge veterinary bill—and a lot of heartache—waiting to happen. Tiny pups happen sometimes by accident, but keep away from someone who intentionally breeds for these dwarf-Poms.

Christmas Puppies

This advice may fly in the face of tradition, your personal wishes, and several other

Christmas puppies are generally a bad idea. So much goes on in a holiday household that a new puppy could easily be neglected.

accepted ideas, but surprising someone with a puppy on Christmas morning is not a good idea. Bringing a new puppy into your home at a time when a lot of hectic activities are planned cannot help an already bewildered puppy adjust to a new environment. Instead, give the puppy several weeks before Christmas or several weeks after Christmas when it can be the center of attention, can get the care it needs and deserves, and can realize that these new people in its life really do love it.

CARING FOR YOUR POMERANIAN

Preparations

A change of environment can be stressful for any dog. For your Pomeranian to have the best possible start in its new home, there are a number of things you can do to make the transition less traumatic.

✔ Purchase a sturdy, flat-bottomed water bowl and a similar one for food. These should not easily turn over and yet should be shallow enough for your Pom to be able to get *at* their contents without having to get *in* with the contents.

✔ You need to obtain some of the exact same food that the puppy has been eating; change brands some other time, if you wish, but definitely not during such a trying time for your new dog.

✔ A dog cage, crate, or carrier (see the chapter on Training, page 81), perhaps of the airline-approved type, will be essential in fulfilling the "den" requirements so important to Pomeranians. This cage, crate, or carrier will be your dog's special place within your home. It will also be a great aid in housebreaking, as we shall soon see.

✔ Your pup will need a collar and lead of appropriate size—or perhaps a one-piece nylon collar and lead—to introduce it to the big, new world.

✔ You should also purchase a good-quality grooming comb and brush. Ask the breeder or pet store to recommend a good brand.

Toys: A very important area where the breeder or pet store may be able to assist is with toys. If your Pom puppy has taken an interest in a particular toy while still at the breeder's, by all means obtain that particular toy. Pomeranians are great little possessors and such a toy would help the pup, or older dog, adjust to its new home with you. If no such special interest in a particular toy has been observed, ask about the kind of toys to get.

If you have chosen a puppy and are yet to take it home, you might introduce such a plaything to your chosen puppy before it is ready to go home so that it will already be familiar. Handle the toy yourself and also have your family members handle the toy so that your scents will not be completely alien to the puppy when the time to go home with you arrives. In any case, toys are essential for Poms.

"Puppy-proofing" Your Home

Another essential is the "puppy-proofing" that must be done before you bring your Pomeranian home. This can be an interesting and enlightening experience for you. In much the same way that you might prepare a room

These very young Poms are just the right age to begin the care and socialization that will turn them into excellent adult companion animals.

for an active toddler, you need to go over all the areas in your home to which the puppy will have access for anything that could do it harm. One dog expert suggests that you actually get down on the floor and check out each room from the puppy's perspective.

Your Pomeranian puppy will have had limited experience outside of that gained through its mother, littermates, and the breeder. You will now have to ensure that this special puppy gets the right learning opportunities it needs to avoid injury through an oversight on your part or puppyish ignorance on its part.

After you have crawled all over the floor seeking potentially dangerous objects, closed-off stairwells and other unsafe places, purchased the things your new puppy will need, reminded all members of the family that having a new puppy, literally underfoot, means new responsibilities, and gone over a list of possible problems and assigned duties, you and the breeder or pet store must work out a time that will be the very best for the puppy to go home with you.

Arrange to be home for the next several days, or have a responsible person at home to help the puppy adjust. You are now ready to bring your Pom puppy home.

Adjustment Period

The Cage/Crate

As mentioned earlier, an important way to help your new Pomeranian adjust to its new home is by purchasing a dog cage, crate, or carrier. As with toys, you might also introduce your new puppy to this new cage, crate, or carrier even *before* you bring the puppy home. By taking this preliminary step, the puppy, or even an older dog, can have its own den with its own familiar scents and comforting sameness before it ever arrives at your home.

Pomeranians love to have their own possessions and can become quite attached to them.

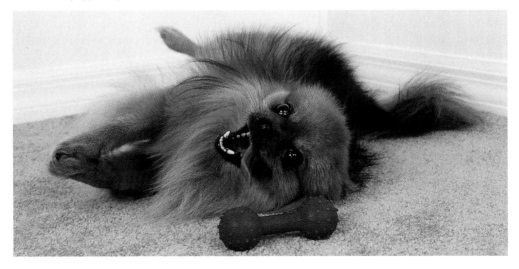

Crate training using an airline carrier like this one or some other cage or crate is an excellent way to housebreak your Pomeranian puppy while providing the Pom with a place of its own within your home.

The importance of such a den to your Pomeranian cannot be overestimated. It will be your pup's own special place, a sanctuary, within your home. Such a place of warmth and safety will be crucial to your puppy's well-being. Some humans mistakenly see this as locking *in* the dog, but the dog sees it as a way to lock the people *out!* In the trying times of adjusting to its new home, this den is a safe haven in a world that the dog may find confusing or even frightening.

There are some steps you can take to make it a little easier on the puppy *within* the crate.

✔ An old-fashioned hot water bottle (nonleaking) or some toy or piece of familiar bedding can be comforting to the pup.

✔ An old wind-up alarm clock, whose ticking may serve to replace the mother's heartbeat, can also be an aid; make sure the alarm portion of this clock is inoperable.

✔ Some have suggested that turning on a radio on low volume to an all-night talk station can be of comfort to the puppy in falling asleep. For tips on crate training, see page 91.

The Ride Home

For an eight-week-old puppy, the actual trip to its new home can be traumatic in itself. If possible, have a member of the family gently hold the puppy, being sure to support the pup's body from beneath while not squeezing it too tightly, during the ride; an old bathrobe and some paper towels might not be a bad idea in the event of motion sickness. If this family member could already be an "old friend" from previous visits to the pup, so much the better. Poms do love to travel, but even a short car ride may be overwhelming to a young pup. Don't get things off to a bad start.

If the journey is several hours or more, frequent stopping for "nature breaks" and to reassure the puppy are a good idea. If the puppy cannot be in someone's arms, it should be in its carrier. Don't allow the puppy to stand up or to attempt to run around inside the car. Unexpected stops, sharp turns, or even falling off the car seat can cause injury.

Beginning Housebreaking

When you arrive home, give your Pomeranian a chance to nose around in the outside

CHECKLIST

Puppy-proofing

✔ You should look for pins, needles, tacks, beads, toxic houseplants, or anything that a small, inquisitive puppy might discover and possibly chew or swallow.

✔ Also be on the lookout for exposed electrical wires or things that, if pulled on by a puppy, might fall on it.

✔ Check for exposed woodwork that, especially in older homes, may have lead-based paint or that may have been treated with some chemical polish or spray that might do harm to a young, teething puppy.

✔ Stairwells and narrow spaces behind appliances or furniture where a puppy might fall or get trapped are obvious danger areas.

✔ Pomeranian puppies don't need to be doing much jumping. Their little legs can so easily break on what might not appear to be any distance at all, as from the sofa to the floor. Damage can also be done to little shoulders and hips. Keep your Pom off the furniture for its sake and the furniture's.

area where you will normally be walking the pup and where you will want it to defecate and urinate. Training begins *now* by not confusing the animal about where you expect it to eliminate. If the puppy relieves itself in the appropriate area, praise it liberally. Pomeranians are smart and it shouldn't take too long for it to associate going outside to this specific location with urination and defecation. This type of patience and consistency on your part will make housebreaking much less of a trauma for both the puppy and you.

Exploring

Assuming you have pup-proofed the areas inside your home where the puppy will be allowed to enter, give your new family member some time to explore. Remember that it is still a puppy and may tire quickly. Certainly play with the puppy, but when it shows signs of tiring, return it to its den. The puppy will soon learn where it is to sleep and may even soon begin to go directly there when it is tired or seeks the comfort of its own place.

Allowing the Pup to Adjust

Your puppy will now have to learn to adjust to being alone without its mother or litter-mates, but *you* will also have to make an adjustment. You are training your Pomeranian by your actions, and rapid learning is taking place in your young dog's fertile mind. If you are intent on crate-training your puppy—using the crate, cage, or carrier to serve as its home-within-the-home—then you must let it know that it will not be allowed out, cuddled, petted, or fawned over when it whines or cries. You can quietly speak to the puppy to reassure it that you are there, but if you do take the puppy into your arms at each cry, it will soon learn how to get into your arms—by crying.

Consistency is vital here. If you are determined, as you should be, not to give in to the wails and whimpers, and some other family member slips in and takes the puppy out of its sleeping place, then all of your resolve is for nothing. No one prefers to listen to a sad, lonely puppy crying, but that puppy can become a sad, lonely adult dog that is still crying if consistent training is not firmly followed. Steel yourself and your family to a few nights of crying with the knowledge that, as with inoculations for disease, a little discomfort now will mean a much happier and better adjusted pet later.

Feeding the New Puppy

Feeding your new puppy should not be too difficult, but again, consistency is important. You have already obtained the very same food that the puppy has been eating. Using this same food, if the breeder was not experiencing some food-related problem with this puppy, on the same schedule to which the puppy is accustomed, will aid in avoiding some of the transitional stress. Even with the same diet, transplanting a puppy will have some negative impact on it. Expect some minor diarrhea for a day or so; see your veterinarian if it continues more than a couple of days, especially when feeding the same diet. Keep on schedule with your pup's feedings. As with a human infant, much of the puppy's first days will be taken up with eating and sleeping. If your puppy is to adapt to its new environment quickly and easily, it will need consistency. You are the source for that.

The development of a good adult Pomeranian begins in the breeding pen and continues in the food bowl. No dog can grow up to meet its potential without high-quality food fed in a consistent manner.

Traveling with Your Pom

Traveling with a Pom is a good deal easier than with some breeds. The Pomeranian is a highly adaptable little dog that enjoys traveling and seems to suffer few side effects from it. Where some dogs are stressed by a change of scenery, the Pom takes it in stride and seems to thrive on it.

There are those Pomeranian breeders who believe that the Pomeranian's good record as a show dog and as an Obedience trial dog comes, at least in part, from its ability to do well in varied environments—its adaptability. Whether the Pom does well in competition on the road because it likes to travel is open to discussion. One thing is for sure: The Pomeranian can make a very good traveling buddy.

Traveling with any pet, even a good traveler like the Pom, calls for some planning and preparations on your part. Since many Poms are crate-trained and can take their den with them, including your dog on your vacation could be a great idea.

Air Travel

Traveling by air with a pet has certainly changed over the years. Today, your Pom and its airline-approved carrier are welcomed on most if not all of the larger domestic and overseas airlines.

Note: If your dog's den is something other than an approved carrier, these are available, for a fee, from the airlines.

Even though conditions are better for the flying pet now, there are still some good rules to follow before your Pom takes off:

1. Well before you make reservations for yourself, check with the airlines about their rules and suggestions for taking your pet along. Some may even let your pet ride in the passenger section with you as carry-on luggage.

2. Check with your pet's veterinarian to see if there are any reasons why your Pom shouldn't make the trip; for instance, very young pups or older dogs might be best left at home. The veterinarian can also provide a health certificate for your dog if the airline requires it, which they usually do and which usually must be dated no more than ten days from the date of your trip. Ask the veterinarian about the need for tranquilizers or anti-airsickness pills for your pet.

3. Make your reservations and those for your pet well in advance of the trip date. If your pet cannot be in the passenger area with you, try to get a direct flight to your destination, even if you have to drive to the nearest hub airport to do so. This will allow you to see your pet loaded on the same plane that you board and lessen the chance of you and your Pomeranian ending up on different planes—or in different cities.

4. If you are traveling to another country, be sure to meet all the entry requirements for bringing in a pet.

5. If using your own airline-approved carrier, carefully check over the carrier to see that none of the screws holding it together have loosened, that the door and latch work effectively, and that it has the necessary airline "conversion kit" for a water dish that can be filled from outside the carrier.

6. Make sure that you have the "Live Animal" stickers prominently displayed on your crate along with a luggage tag with your name, your home telephone number, and a number where you can be reached in your destination city.

7. Be sure to enclose in the carrier a freshly laundered pad or blanket to make the carrier more comfortable. A favorite toy would be a nice addition.

8. Do not feed your pet for eight to ten hours prior to departure. You can, however, give it water and exercise up to two hours before boarding. Other than the external water dish, don't put food or water in the carrier. It will only be a potential mess.

Note: Make sure you have packed in your luggage enough of your Pom's regular food and any medications it may need during the trip.

9. Have your firm but polite demeanor ready to make sure that airline personnel realize how important your Pomeranian is to you and to what lengths you will go to ensure its safety and comfort. One frequent flyer dog breeder makes a point of taking a picture of the dog in its crate as it is being readied for loading on the flight. She claims that the existence of such photographic proof has helped her avoid many problems.

Car Travel

You will make many short trips with your Pomeranian in a private automobile. While the requirements for taking your dog with you on a longer trip in your car are not as stringent as those of an airline, you would do well not to take these extended car travel precautions too lightly.

1. Always have your Pomeranian in a carrier or in a doggy safety harness when you are riding together.

2. Check with the veterinarian for some motion sickness medications; don't feed your Pom 8 to 12 hours before you plan to leave, and provide it water only up to two hours before leaving.

3. Stop every hour or so to give the dog a breather, a drink of water, and some exercise.

4. Always use your lead when you take the dog out of the carrier.

5. *Never* leave your dog in a parked car, even with windows rolled down, during the day when the temperature is as high as 60°F (16°C) (see heatstroke, page 76).

6. If you are traveling across the country, check with auto clubs and travel guides about which motels and hotels allow pets in their rooms. You might also confirm that they allow well-behaved pets when you make reservations by phone. A little planning will make the trip safer and saner.

7. Avoid "pet walks" at rest areas if you have a very young puppy that could pick up a disease from such a location.

Boarding Your Pom

If you can't take your pet with you on your trip, then boarding it will be your alternative. This is not as bleak a prospect as you might think. There are several good possibilities.

Most Pomeranians are good travelers.

1. In many locales, pet sitters are available to take care of your pet in your own home while you are away. Usually these are skillful, caring people who can furnish numerous valid references.

2. You and your Pom may have a friend, neighbor, or family member who can care for your pet. Your dog might be able to stay at home under this arrangement. This person needs to be someone the Pomeranian likes.

3. Your veterinarian or your groomer may board dogs and would be already known and accepted by your dog in a place it knows.

4. The breeder where you bought your Pom, if nearby, may be willing to take an alumnus in as a boarder, in which circumstance you will be sure of good care.

5. There are some excellent boarding kennels that are accredited with the American Boarding Kennel Association (ABKA) (see page 92).

FEEDING YOUR POMERANIAN

A Balanced Diet

You have gone to considerable effort to learn about and obtain a good-quality Pomeranian. What you feed your Pom will be a major factor in its health, both mental and physical, and in its longevity. The importance of a balanced diet and your understanding of what makes it balanced will be a key to this important part of dog ownership.

The computer phrase "garbage in; garbage out" is also an apt point to remember about canine nutrition. Your Pomeranian will need a balanced diet to grow strong and healthy, and to develop the potential that is its genetic birthright. A poor diet can cause your Pom a legion of medical, behavioral, and developmental problems.

Avoiding a poor diet and establishing a solid nutritional plan isn't difficult. Provide your Pomeranian with a high-quality dog food and *don't overfeed*.

Basic Nutrition

There are seven components to a balanced diet for your Pomeranian: proteins, carbohydrates, fats, vitamins, minerals, water, and consistency/knowledge.

This pet-quality Pomeranian is standing tall for a treat. Although this is a cute trick, it should be discouraged at the dinner table. Remember that too many treats can make a slender dog like this pudgy and fat.

Protein

Protein provides the dog with amino acids that are essential for growth, the maintenance of healthy muscle and bone, the repair of that same muscle and bone, the production of infection-fighting antibodies, and production of hormones and enzymes that aid in the dog's body's chemical processes. Good sources of protein are meat and poultry products, milk products, fish meal, and corn.

Carbohydrates

Carbohydrates provide energy to power the Pom's internal motor. Thoroughly cooked grains, starches, and vegetables provide most of the carbohydrates seen in quality dog foods. Carbohydrates are measured in calories.

Fats

Fat is another much more concentrated source of energy for your Pomeranian, which can provide more than twice as much energy as a like amount of protein or carbohydrates. Fat also provides the "delivery system" for the fat-soluble vitamins, A, D, E, and K, into your Pom's system for healthy skin and coat. In addition, fat aids in maintaining a healthy nervous system and makes dog food taste better.

Vitamins

Vitamins are needed for general body functions and generally needed in small quantities that are easily provided in a balanced diet of a high-quality dog food so that additional supplementation is *not* usually needed. The best source of vitamins is a well-balanced diet.

Minerals

Minerals are essential for normal body functioning: Calcium and phosphorus are needed for strong bones, muscles, and teeth; potassium and sodium aid in the maintenance of a healthy nervous system and in the maintenance of normal bodily fluids; iron promotes healthy blood in your pet by transporting oxygen throughout its body.

Important note: A high-quality dog food will contain the appropriate levels of both vitamins and minerals. Don't try to supplement a high-quality dog food without first consulting with your veterinarian. Both vitamins and minerals can be easily overdone.

Water

Water is often the most neglected part of a dog's diet, yet it is a very important component. Your Pom will need plenty of clean, fresh water all the time. It might not hurt—you or your dog—if you had your water tested annually even if you are part of a municipal water system. With water purity a question in many communities, your actions here may be a good preventative against chemical imbalances or interactions.

Consistency/Knowledge

Another often-ignored aspect of a balanced diet is the manner in which you provide food to your dog. As with so many other areas of Pom care, consistency is important in diet as well. Find a good high-quality dog food that your pet likes and stay with it. Even experienced dog people, who should know better, often buy one type of food, then they switch to another type, without regard for the dog's needs. Changing from one food source to another should usually take two weeks or longer with the gradual mixing of the new food with the old in ever-increasing amounts until the old is gone.

You knowledge about canine nutrition and about dog foods is very important to the health of your Pomeranian, who has to depend on you.

Commercial Dog Food

Commercial dog foods generally come in three forms: dry, semimoist, and canned. There are a number of excellent high-quality dog foods on the market today, and an even greater number of inferior products trying to

As important as a high-quality food is, fresh, clean water is equally important. Abundant water is even more important if your pet is fed an exclusively dry dog food diet.

If you feed a high-quality, premium dog food, no vitamin and mineral supplementation is usually needed. Before you add any supplements to a dog's food, check with your veterinarian.

capture your attention and dog food dollars. As with finding the right Pomeranian for you, the adage "You get what you pay for" relates just as well to dog food. If you will take time to learn some basic facts about dog foods, you'll ultimately save money while providing a high-quality, balanced diet for your Pom.

Labels

The first thing to learn is how to read a dog food label. Look at the list of ingredients. These ingredients are listed by rank of percentage of the total product that each represents. For example, if "chicken, corn, rice . . ." are listed as the first three ingredients in a particular dog food, then chicken is the largest single ingredient in the food, with corn being the next highest in percentage, rice being the third highest, and so on, down the list of ingredients.

Normally, the first three or four items will combine to make up as much as 85 percent of the dog food, with the long list of additional ingredients making up the remaining 15 percent. Some companies play games with their ingredient lists by breaking down some items into several separate listings in order to change the percentage these appear to have in the list of ingredients. A dog food might truly have corn as its main ingredient with chicken next in line and someone in marketing might decide that a poultry-based food might be easier to market. Look out for food manufacturers that do this to make their product look different than it really

is. The manufacturers of really high-quality or "premium" dog foods don't resort to this tactic.

Another thing to read on the label is the maker's recommended feeding amounts for a dog the size of your Pom. Generally, these are broad recommendations and may or may not fit your dog. You will, possibly with your veterinarian's help, soon learn the best amount to feed your Pomeranian.

The manufacturers of the better dog foods will have a toll-free telephone number that you can use to inquire about their products. Use this number! Find a company that will let you talk to a pet nutritionist or staff veterinarian. Ask questions about the food and about any Pomeranian test information they may have. Most of the better companies welcome questions and have skillful members available to help you with your dog food questions.

Premium dog food will not generally be available in grocery stores. It is usually avail-

This pet-quality Pom is showing its ability to entice its owner to give treats. Some treats are fine, but care must be taken that too many tasty morsels do not upset the balance of the dog's regular diet. Table scraps are always inappropriate as treats.

Also, a quality dry dog food will help clean your dog's teeth and gums. Dry dog food is the most economical way to feed a premium dog food. It is easy to feed, easy to store, with no refrigeration needed to keep it fresh. Premium dry dog foods are high in palatability and digestibility, producing smaller and firmer stools. Your dog actually eats less and gets more from a premium food. Dry dog food has about 10 percent moisture, so be certain you keep plenty of clean, fresh water available to your Pom. Also, remember to feed a dry food that is small enough for your Pom to easily eat.

Semimoist Food

Semimoist food comes in burgers or in other shaped versions. It is very palatable and convenient. It is generally more expensive than dry food and contains approximately 30 percent moisture. Stools are usually less firm with semimoist dog food than with dry dog food.

Canned Food

Canned food is the most expensive dog food. It is quite palatable, but due to its high water content (approximately 75 percent) it can quickly spoil, even at room temperature. A tendency exists among dogs that are fed canned food to overeat, which can lead to obesity and other problems. Stools are not firm with canned food and some foods produce particularly foul-smelling excretions.

able from veterinarians, pet stores, through better general feed stores, or some groomers. For your Pomeranian, premium-quality dog food may be a little more expensive, but it will be well worth it in terms of better health for your dog.

Dry Food

There are a number of advantages to a high-quality dry dog food. Most importantly, there are several dry foods that can truthfully call themselves "nutritionally complete." As such they will be the balanced diet you are seeking.

Homemade Diets

Unless you are a trained animal nutritionist with access to all the foods that will be needed for a balanced diet, this approach is best left alone. Your Pom will need a complete nutrition program and such a program is available in high-quality dog food from several companies that have spent multimillions to make it available to you for your dog.

Treats

Leave table scraps off your Pomeranian's menu. If you don't start the habit of feeding the dog items from your plate, begging can be avoided. Also, table scraps aren't part of your goal—a nutritionally complete and balanced diet. A dog will often neglect its regular food in favor of treats and scraps.

There are some excellent dog biscuits available that are nutritionally complete and have the added bonus of helping to clean your dog's teeth and gums and give it a nutritional "chew" at the same time. Treats need to be apportioned with care lest they unbalance the balanced diet that you are trying to maintain.

If you feed a high-quality dry dog food, there is one trick you can use to give your pet a treat and some variety without throwing off the balanced diet. Put a small amount of your Pom's dry food in a microwave-safe bowl. Add a teaspoon or two of water to the dry food. Microwave on high for about 30 seconds and allow the food to cool. The nutrients remain the same, but the fats in the dry food are pulled toward the surface. This will give the Pom the same food with a little different taste, not unlike the difference in a charcoal-broiled hamburger and one cooked on the stove. Don't use too much water on the dry dog food or you'll interfere with stool firmness.

This method, with a little more water, is helpful in feeding older dogs with teeth problems where a softer diet is needed.

Feeding Requirements

Puppies

In order to get your puppy off to the best possible start, for the first year of its life you will need a nutritionally complete balanced diet designed specifically for the needs of growing puppies. Puppies generally need twice as much in the way of nutrition than do adult dogs. Feed it the best high-quality puppy food available and you shouldn't run into any problems. The key is to start your Pom puppy on the right nutritional diet from the very beginning. Try to find a puppy diet, if you are changing, in a size that will be easily handled by a small-breed puppy such as the Pomeranian. Several premium dry foods fit this requirement. A puppy under six months old should be fed three or four times daily. At six months, cut back to two or three times daily, depending on the individual needs of the dog.

Adult Dogs

When your Pomeranian reaches physical maturity at around one year, its nutritional needs will change from those of a growing puppy into those of an adult. Two feedings per day will generally suffice as your Pom achieves its mature weight. Other than with added activities such as breeding, showing, Agility, or Obedience work, your Pom's nutritional needs should remain fairly constant for the next six or seven years. Of course, spaying or neutering your pet will change its nutritional requirements to more like those of an older dog.

Older Dogs

When your Pom gets older, its metabolic rate will slow down and it will need less energy, and thus less fat and protein. It is important that the older Pomeranian of eight years or more not gain too much weight. This is also true of the spayed and neutered Pom even before it has reached eight years of age.

One of the hardest things to convince dog owners of is that an older dog doesn't need the same amount of food it did when it was younger. "But Buffy always gets two cups of dog food" is the commonly heard reply when food reduction is suggested. Buffy's owner is not helping her live a long and healthy life by continuing to feed her the same amount she ate when she was much younger.

Many of the premium dog foods now have foods designed for the less active metabolism of older dogs or for spayed and neutered dogs. Contact your veterinarian or the company that makes the dog food you have been using. (This would be a good time to take advantage of the 800 number of your premium dog food company.)

Finding the right diet for your Pom can help avoid potential ailments.

A Feeding Trial

Finding a balanced diet for your Pomeranian that it likes isn't that difficult. Perhaps you can find a veterinarian who has taken a special interest in canine nutrition. Become a label reader and ask lots of questions of the dog food companies. An aware consumer is a good consumer and your efforts will pay off for you and your Pomeranian.

Always consult with your veterinarian on special dietetic problems that afflict some dogs; however, a good balanced diet program from puppyhood on should help your Pom avoid many ailments. Find a high-quality food and stick with it. If the product isn't doing what you think it should, follow this simple feeding trial:

✔ Always compare apples to apples. Don't put a canned or semimoist food up against a dry food, for example.

✔ Obtain one sample of a new food that you believe might give you the results you desire. Put it in a dog dish near your pet's regular food. If the dog shows interest in the new food, let it eat an amount that is the equivalent of the regular amount you normally feed. Your dog may eat some of each or spurn the new food altogether. Don't let a piggish Pom eat more than it should regularly have.

✔ If your dog likes the new food, follow the gradual-shift practice of mixing the old with the new until the new food is in place.

✔ Monitor stool firmness and volume, coat and skin condition, and the overall appearance of your pet.

✔ If the new food passes all the tests after a month or so of trial, you may have found a product to stay with.

Changing Foods

Don't be constantly seeking to change foods. If your current premium food is doing all the things you want with regard to stools, hair, skin, and so forth, stay with it. Change your premium food when conditions dictate that a change is needed. Don't change because you like another food's bag color, its ads on TV, or its lowered sale price. The food your pet eats is crucial to its well-being and should not be casually changed as one might change brands of gasoline.

If you do change to a premium food and there is some hesitation on your Pom's part in continuing to eat it, give the food a chance. Feed the new food in your usual manner. If the dog does not eat it, remove the food until the next regular feeding and give nothing else. Missing one feeding won't hurt most adult Pomeranians, and once a dog starts to eat a food, it begins to like it. Your dog will normally eat less of a premium food because it takes less of this food to meet the dog's nutritional needs; this will also make the best premium food more economical in the long run than any cheap, bargain brand.

The kind of care that the puppy receives will largely determine what kind of adult it will become.

TIP

Health Indicators
The food bowl is a good health indicator. Pay attention to the dog's eating habits. You may get an early warning to some ailment or physical condition that needs your veterinarian's attention. Also pay attention to the dog's bowel movements, another good health indicator.

Food Allergies

Some dogs will develop allergic reactions to certain foods. Your veterinarian can help you recognize such allergies, isolate the cause, and find a diet that your dog's system can handle.

GROOMING YOUR POMERANIAN

An Overview

The Pomeranian is not a difficult dog to keep well groomed, but there are certain coat considerations that must be taken into account. Even though the Pom is a toy breed, its ancestry is northern. The Pomeranian, according to the AKC Standard (see pages 17–19) should have a coat of the following description:

Double coated, a short, soft, thick undercoat, with longer, coarse glistening outercoat consisting of guard hairs that must be harsh to the touch in order to give the proper texture for the coat to form a frill of profuse, spreading straight hairs.

There are almost as many opinions about Pomeranian grooming as there are Pomeranian breeders, but one thing is very clear. The exacting requirements for a show dog are different than the needs of the average dog owner who has a Pom for a pet.

Grooming Show Poms

A show Pomeranian will require an excellent coat tended in a careful, consistent manner. If you are serious about pursuing a show career for your Pom, the most direct course will be

This little boy and this Pomeranian are friends. Such a relationship is good for the dog and the boy and makes grooming much easier.

the wisest. You have, of course, purchased a puppy from the best show stock available from the best available breeder. Go to this breeder and ask questions about show grooming. If this is not possible, find the Pomeranian exhibitor whose dogs evidence the best coats and the best show preparation. Pay this person whatever he or she asks for lessons on how to make a Pomeranian show-ready. Listen, learn, and follow his or her advice. But also remember, if exhibiting your Pomeranian is your goal, then no amount of external preparation can put a good coat on a dog whose breeding hasn't put the potential there for a good coat.

Grooming Pet Poms

For the pet Pom owner, grooming holds no great mystery. Grooming tools for a Pomeranian consist of a good brush with natural bristles and a fine slicker brush or comb for the head, ear, and skirts. About twice a week or so, gently brush your Pomeranian to keep its coat looking good. Brush away, or against the lay of the coat. Follow up with a fine-tooth comb on skirts and neck.

Groomers

About twice a year or perhaps quarterly (as included in the Pom budget, previously mentioned), take your Pomeranian to a good,

professional dog groomer. Depending on your dog's special needs, a bath, a flea dip, or both may or may not be needed. The groomer will know how to keep your Pomeranian looking good. The groomer will also attend to hair trimming in the areas of the neck, feet, anus, and anal glands, and will keep the toenails at an appropriate length.

If you find that you enjoy grooming your own Pom, which many pet owners do not, learn what you must do and be consistent about it. Every exhibitor should certainly know how to show-groom his or her own dog but, for a pet owner, grooming sessions are usually done by a professional groomer. If you don't know a respected groomer, ask your veterinarian or pet store to recommend one.

Pomeranians need regular grooming all their lives if they are to look their best. As with so many aspects of pet ownership, grooming should always begin very early in a puppy's life.

Using a professional groomer on a semiannual basis will pay off in other than grooming-related areas: A groomer can spot parasite problems, skin conditions, and other concerns that you might miss at home. Your groomer, along with your regular veterinarian, will make up a team that will keep things pleasant and healthy for your Pomeranian's teeth, ears, eyes, and nails. A good groomer can be a great aid to you in caring for your Pomeranian. Take time to find the best possible groomer, and

These two Poms, an orange and a cream, are beautifully groomed and look like they are ready for a night on the town.

encourage an active interest in your Pom. Take the groomer's advice as that of a professional who wants the best for your pet.

Regular visits to the groomer, who may be affiliated with a veterinarian, a quality pet store, or a grooming shop, will also serve two other purposes. First, your Pomeranian will enjoy getting out and seeing new things. This is a good opportunity for a trip with a purpose. Second, it will be good for you to have a chance to see new dog care products, toys, or other items that

may interest you. You can also take some pride in your Pomeranian and in the care you have provided. A little showing off never hurts.

Start Early

As with most other aspects of the Pomeranian, an early introduction to brushing and grooming is best for the Pom puppy so that your dog will not fear or dislike these activities. Begin as early as possible to help your puppy learn that daily brushing can be a pleasant time for both of you.

As a young puppy, take your Pom to your chosen groomer and introduce it not only to the groomer but to the sights, sounds, and smells of the place. Groomers will often take

The basic grooming tools needed to keep a Pomeranian's coat in good condition are wire and bristle brushes, a wire slicker brush, a comb with medium and fine teeth, a tangle remover, nail clippers, an electric clipper, and a grooming glove.

time to place a clipper next to the puppy and let it feel the warmth and vibration while being gently held. This works wonders in helping to avoid fear later on.

Pom Coat Phases

It is important to know that all Poms go through phases when their coats are not at their best. The fluffy puppy you bought at seven or eight weeks of age will usually begin to radically shed its coat when it is about four months old and the coat will look ragged.

The adult coat will begin to show up at about six months of age, as will evidence of the pup's adult color. The adult coat may hold on up to about a year, when normally your Pom will shed its coat and look ragged again. This is especially true of male Poms. Females tend to shed in conjunction with their coming into season. Brood bitches with puppies also tend to lose their coats, a point to remember when looking at the mother of your prospective puppy, as she may not look as good as she normally does.

Regular weekly brushing will keep these shedding periods easier to manage. A puppy that has been taught to enjoy the regular brushing sessions will not be difficult to handle when shedding makes brushing all the more important.

TIP

Partial Bath

A useful technique that many Pomeranian owners use is the partial bath that can be given a couple of times a week: Using a warm, damp washcloth, wash the underside of your dog and make sure that no fecal material has adhered to the hair around the anus. This is especially useful in keeping the urine smell off the penis and surrounding area of your male Pomeranian.

With the regular care of a good professional groomer, your frequent brushing, and your touch-up cleaning a couple of times a week, your Pomeranian will stay in presentable shape. You will want your dog to look good.

This black Pom puppy is waiting patiently for just the right owner to come along.

RAISING QUALITY POMERANIANS

Responsibilities

Unless you are realistic about the prospects of becoming a breeder of Pomeranians, perhaps you should skip this chapter. Because only a tiny percentage of Pomeranians are good enough to be designated breeding stock, only a few Pom owners or potential owners are good candidates to be Pomeranian breeders. Don't be offended if this chapter changes your mind about becoming a Pom breeder. Be glad.

The self-searching introspection that is required before you buy a Pomeranian is needed even more before you decide to be a breeder of Pomeranians. A good question to ask is: "Why do I want to raise Pomeranians?" If your answer to this question is to let your bitch have the experience of having puppies, save her some trouble. Many Pomeranian bitches have real difficulty in whelping, and cesarean sections are commonly needed. Some little females are too small to successfully produce a litter of puppies and can die trying.

If your answer is motivated by some imagined pot of gold at the end of a Pomeranian rainbow, forget it. For every person who makes a dollar raising dogs, there are many who spend thousands in the same pursuit. Moreover, unless you are out of touch with the real world, you know that there are many more

Only the best-quality Pomeranians should be candidates for the breeding pen.

puppies born than there are responsible owners to care for them. Why add to the problem?

Another point to ponder before embarking on a breeding enterprise is this: Are you willing to take responsibility for any and all puppies you cause to be born—for their *entire* lives? They didn't ask to be brought into the world; you did it. You must own up to it. It is not uncommon for dog breeders to sell (or give) a good puppy to an apparently wonderful home, only to find that the puppy is mistreated, requiring it to be reclaimed and placed in another home, or sometimes even mercifully be put to sleep. Breeders go through that experience far too often.

If raising Poms is a sort of status thing based on some personal ego-bolstering need, buy a really good Pomeranian puppy and campaign it to an AKC championship or to an Obedience ring degree. That's where the status is with dogs, and you'll even have some fun doing it—if your ego can stand any setbacks you may encounter.

If, after falling in love with Pomeranians, you feel that you would like to make a serious effort to improve the breed, then you may have some basis to consider becoming a Pomeranian breeder.

✔ Talk to the breeders you've met. Meet others. Listen to them.

✔ Read and study all you can about canine genetics and dog breeding.

✔ Read the Pomeranian Breed Standard until you can quote it line for line.

✔ Examine your bankbook and then rethink the whole deal.

✔ If you still want to breed Poms, start small with a clear understanding of the pedigrees, genetics, and possible problems involved.

Striving to produce better and better dogs is not an easy undertaking. Meet as many dog breeders as you can. Listen to their stories of failure and success, or achievement and sacrifice before you give serious thought to joining their ranks. The pursuit of excellence, which is the only valid reason to breed dogs, is not without its costs.

Breeding Approaches

There are as many approaches to breeding Pomeranians as there are Pomeranian breeders. Choosing which family or stud dog will help you achieve the ideal you are seeking tends to be a matter of personal conviction. There are, however, three primary approaches that dog breeders, and other animal breeders, take: inbreeding, linebreeding, and outcrossing.

Inbreeding

Inbreeding is the mating of close relatives: brothers and sisters, fathers and daughters, mothers and sons. The purpose of inbreeding is to intensify the genetic makeup of these close relatives in their offspring. The hope is that the good qualities will become that much stronger and easier to pass on to coming generations.

This is called *fixing type,* which means that you would have a family (or line) in which there would be no bad qualities sneaking in to mess up your plans for that perfect Pom. It is true that inbreeding has the capability of fixing type on the good attributes; there is, however, another side to inbreeding: Inbreeding is just an approach, not an automatic way to perfection. If inbreeding can intensify the good, it can also intensify the bad. Because of this double-edged sword that cuts both ways in the none-too-apparent world of dog genetics, inbreeding is best left to the experts.

Linebreeding

Linebreeding is again the mating of related dogs, but not close relatives as in inbreeding. Nephew to aunt, niece to uncle, cousin to cousin are examples of linebreeding. The goal is the same as inbreeding. Linebreeders hope to build up the good genes while cutting down on the bad genes.

It is because of the distance between these relatives that linebreeding is somewhat slower than inbreeding in achieving success; but again, linebreeding is also much slower in causing failure.

Outcrossing

In the strictest sense of the word, outcrossing would be the mating of dogs of totally dissimilar breeds, such as a Pom and a Pug, for example. This is actually called *crossbreeding.* Outcrossing would be taking a Pomeranian from a famous English family of Poms and breeding it to a member of a famous American family of Poms that have no close common ancestry with the English family in any generation. The outcross might do well or what breeders call "nick." They would say that the English dog "nicked" with the American dog. This would mean, at least for the first generation, that the specimens would be quite good, perhaps better than either parent.

This beautiful Pomeranian female is a good candidate for breeding, but only to a stud dog that can complement her genetic heritage.

The goal of inbreeding and linebreeding is to limit the number of genes, and therefore the amount of difference, in the family or "strain." The purpose of outcrossing is to introduce new genes, possibly in an attempt to correct some condition in the strain. For example, Pom Strain A has excellent size, type (shape), and color, but the coat quality leaves much to be desired. You, as the Pom breeder, have studied other strains (B, C, D, E, and so forth) and have decided that Strain B would be a likely source of new genetic material in your dogs. You chose B because even though this strain has some weaknesses in size and other areas, it produces superb coats. The ultimate goal of this outcross is to produce offspring that will retain the good A qualities of size, type, and color *combined* with the excellent coat qualities of B. You may reach that goal on the first cross, but then again you may not. You may end up with puppies that have all the coat qualities of A (weak at best) with the size, type, and color of B (also weak). Since this was a pure outcross, you may have, if you breed this long enough, every range in each quality from very bad to very good.

Outcrossing, like inbreeding, is best left to the pros. If you decide to breed Poms, take your time and follow the lead of the more experienced breeders that you have met.

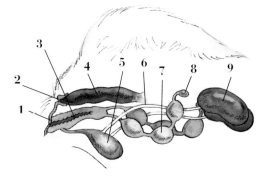

The reproductive system of a female dog.

1. *vulva*
2. *anus*
3. *vagina*
4. *rectum*
5. *bladder*
6. *ureter*
7. *developing embryo*
8. *ovaries*
9. *kidneys*

The Estrous Cycle

Female Poms usually come into "heat," or season, two times a year beginning at approximately six months. These heat cycles can last up to three weeks. The entire reproductive cycle is called *estrous,* and consists of four stages. Each stage has its own purpose and its own signs, although these are sometimes blurred and go out of one stage and into another. Each stage is part of the reproductive life of a dog.

Proestrus: The first stage, called *proestrus,* marks the beginning of activity within the uterus and the ovaries. The ovaries produce eggs, or *ova.* As these ova mature, the uterine wall becomes thicker. The external genitalia get larger. A blood-tinged discharge from the vagina becomes noticeable. This stage will last from 9 to 14 days. During this stage, males are attracted to the female, but she is not ready to mate with them.

Estrus: *Estrus,* the next stage, not to be confused with estrous—the entire cycle—is next in line. The vaginal discharge will become clearer and thicker. Ovulation, usually between the ninth and fourteenth day following the start of the cycle, takes place during estrus, which may last as long as nine days; mating and conception can occur at this time.

Metestrus (also called diestrus): If your female Pom mated and conceived during estrus, her reproductive organs will now begin to adapt—mammary growth for example—for the birth of the puppies.

Anestrus: Anestrus signals the end of metestrus and the completion of the estrous cycle for another half year. If your Pom female did not mate and conceive, her reproductive organs will gradually return to their normal non-heat appearance.

Note: During all of the estrous cycle, your Pomeranian female should be kept away from breeding-age males, including older male puppies. During this time, make every effort to protect her from an unwanted pregnancy.

The Stud

As with so many other aspects of the Pomeranian, the search for a sire, or stud dog, should begin well in advance of the projected mating time. Wisely, you have studied the pedigrees of your dam and of several potential sires. After careful consideration and consultation with seasoned breeders, hopefully you have chosen a male that will blend his genetic qualities with those of your female and that possesses no open (overt) or hidden (covert) defects or flaws that he can pass on to the puppies. This stud dog should be at least one year old, and since your female is a virgin, it is preferable that, when possible, the male has been used as a stud dog before. Usually the male will breed better at home; therefore, the female generally goes to him.

You should have your female—and the stud as well—checked by a veterinarian for the presence of a venereally transmitted bacterial disease known as brucellosis, which can wreak havoc with breeding specimens, sometimes causing aborted litters or sterility. Most serious breeders will require a brucellosis-free statement from a veterinarian about the bitch.

Stud Fee and Arrangement

You would be wise to have the stud fee—payment for the male's mating with your female—clearly spelled out in writing. Most stud dog owners will want a set fee or their pick of the puppies as payment. Since most Pomeranian litters are very small (one to three puppies) and the pick of the litter might be the only show prospect, if you have even one, the straight payment of the fee may be best for you.

You will also want to have an arrangement for another mating if your female fails to conceive after the mating. Usually the owner of the stud dog will guarantee that your bitch will conceive or she can be mated again to the same male at her next heat.

You may want to be present when the mating takes place. If you do not know the stud owner well, you want to be sure that the exact Pomeranian male you want as the sire of your puppies is the one doing the servicing.

If your Pomeranian is not an excellent, show-quality specimen, the stud dog owner may

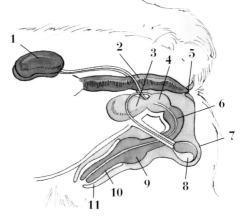

The reproductive system of a male dog.

1. kidneys	*7. scrotum*
2. rectum	*8. testes*
3. bladder	*9. bulb*
4. prostate	*10. penis*
5. anus	*11. sheath*
6. urethra	

refuse to let your female be mated to his or her male. This is a good attitude for a stud dog owner to take. If your female is likely to produce poor-quality puppies, the desirability of the stud dog as a breeder can be lessened. The better your female, the better the chances for producing that outstanding puppy that will enhance the demand for the stud dog. This makes starting with the very best all the more important.

Mating

Since you have been considering this mating for many months, you will have your female in good health prior to the onset of the estrous cycle. Have your veterinarian's approval before you breed her and have her wormed and up to date on her vaccinations.

Give the male and the female Pomeranians a chance to get used to one another before the mating. If possible, use a previously bred male for your female's first mating.

mality rather than exposure to a male can bring on this reaction. Sometimes, false pregnancy is not just a harmless condition. It can be an indicator of pyometritis, which can result in sterility or may require an ovariohysterectomy. Consult your veterinarian if false pregnancy occurs.

Note: Some little Pom females have adopted another female's puppies or even kittens, or have treated a favorite toy like a puppy during the seven or eight weeks this condition lasts.

As mentioned, the ovulating phase of the estrous cycle is when your female can be mounted. Breeders generally try to schedule the mating (or matings) on the ninth and twelfth days after the onset of heat.

The "Tie"

When copulating, the male and female may be "tied" or locked together by the action of the penis and vagina. This is a natural manifestation and will cease when the mating urges subside. Your female can become tied with the stud dog more than once during the two or so days of maximum receptibility, or she may mate with another dog after the initial mating has taken place, so keep her from other males until after estrous has ended.

False Pregnancy

Some nonpregnant Pomeranian females may show all the outward signs of pregnancy; this will sometimes even happen to the tiny, "teacup" Poms for whom normal pregnancy and whelping would be impossible. Hormonal abnor-

Pregnancy

The regular gestation period for an impregnated bitch will be approximately 63 days after the mating, but generally a little less for Pomeranians. At about six weeks of the nine-week period she will begin to show pregnancy, with her abdomen becoming larger and her teats becoming enlarged.

Your Pomeranian dam (mother dog) will need tender loving care during this time, especially if it is her first litter. You should have been feeding her a nutritionally complete diet and she should be heavy with pups, not heavy with excess fat. Her exercise need not be eliminated, but should not be strenuous. You should separate her from other dogs during the last couple of weeks before the puppies are born. You should alert the children not to pick her up and she should have her "den" nearby for her emotional well-being.

Whelping

The Whelping Box

Introduce the dam to the whelping box, which is a box tall enough so that she won't be jumping in and out, yet large enough for her to have plenty of space. The box needs to be in a quiet place where your Pom feels comfortable. Encourage her to use the whelping box for dozing and at night just prior to delivery day. Make sure you have safe bedding that will not allow a tiny puppy to be smothered down in some folds somewhere. The dam's comfort and relaxation are crucial prior to actual whelping. A heat source such as a light or heating pad should be available to keep the puppies warm.

Preparations

Some Pom breeders have the hair around the dam's nipples and vulva trimmed; others reject the idea. Any long hair on her back legs that could wrap around and strangle a puppy should definitely be removed. As whelping time approaches, she may become restless and ill at ease and stop eating. She will fuss with the bedding in the whelping box. At this time, keep her quiet and as comfortable as possible.

While dogs have been having puppies without the help of humans for thousands of years, your Pomeranian will need your rapt attention, especially if this is her first litter. If you are the least bit unsure about this whole experience, or this is your first job as a birthing attendant, you would do well to move your bitch and her whelping box to the veterinarian's office before she gets too close to whelping time. You might also get an experienced breeder—someone your Pom likes and trusts—to help you.

If your Pomeranian dam is a show prospect—as she probably should be if you have decided to breed her—she will be close to the small size required for a show dog. Her size and the compact body of a show-quality Pom can lead to serious birthing problems; therefore, you need to be prepared. If your bitch has labored strenuously for more than two hours without success, a cesarean may be necessary to save her life or to save the lives of the puppies. You should have your veterinarian on call.

The possibility of birthing problems is something you should take into account when you decide to breed Pomeranians. If you have little or no experience in this area, by all means use your veterinarian.

✔ Given an uncomplicated delivery, the mother should pull away the placenta as soon as the puppy is born. She should begin nosing, licking, and cleaning the puppy. It is this action, the nudging and licking, that actually stimulates the new puppy to

This Pomeranian youngster is the result of hundreds of generations of highly selective matings. Purchasing such a puppy and then failing to give it adequate affection and care is a true waste.

Pomeranians normally are good mothers and are very attentive to their puppies. Pomeranian litters are usually quite small, with three puppies considered a large litter.

whimpering, restlessness, and low temperature or body weight can signal feeding problems. Your bitch may not be producing enough milk, or there may be some other difficulty.

Temperature and Feeding

Under normal conditions, puppies grow and develop quickly. Generally, you will have three or fewer puppies so you can easily monitor their progress—imagine what your efforts would have to be if you had one of the larger breeds whose litter can number a dozen or more. If your Pomeranian bitch will not or cannot feed her puppies, you will have to do so. The puppies will need to be kept in a warm place for the first 14 days; the temperature should be kept between 85 and 90°F (29–32°C). After the 14-day period, it can be gradually decreased to 75°F (24°C). Both overheating and chilling can be harmful to the puppies. Use a regular weather thermometer in good working condition to monitor their environment.

For hand-feeding your puppies, follow your veterinarian's recommendations as to what milk replacement to use—Esbilac is one brand name—and how to feed. Remember that Pom puppies are tiny at birth. Use an eyedropper or one of the bottles developed to feed small animals, available from your veterinarian or pet store. Warm the milk to between 95 and 100°F (35–38°C). Feed the puppies as much as they will eat. A good indicator is the absence of whimpering and the presence of little round, full bellies. A newborn puppy should be fed

begin breathing. Pom puppies are truly tiny, weighing between 3 and 5 ounces (85–142 g) with some as small as 1 ounce (28 g) on record.

✔ Your Pom female usually will eat the afterbirth, thus severing the umbilical cord. If she fails to pull away the placental membranes and free the puppy from the sac where it has been nurtured while in the womb, you should move in immediately to help her.

✔ After you clean away the membranes, clear the puppy's airway of any mucus. Rub the puppy gently with a towel or washcloth, simulating the mother's licking and nuzzling.

✔ If no immediate problems exist, carefully transport the mother Pom and her puppies to the veterinarian to assess their health and ascertain if the dam has sufficient colostrum-rich mother's milk to get them off to a good start and to feed them. If your puppies have dewclaws, they can be removed at this time.

Puppy Care

Your puppies must be kept warm and receive enough milk. A healthy puppy will be warm, sleep a lot, and seldom whimper. Be alerted if your puppies don't fit that picture. Constant about every four hours on a regular basis. As they grow, you will be able to lengthen the period between feedings. Follow your veterinarian's advice on this.

Don't leave food or water in the whelping box. Remember that even a relatively shallow drinking bowl can be deep enough to drown a small, uncoordinated Pomeranian puppy. As your puppies begin to eat more and more of the puppy food, decrease the food to the mother. Her milk supply will gradually subside.

The New Mother

Normally, your little Pomeranian female will be a good mother and, barring birthing problems brought on by her small size, she should be able to do the job nicely. Keep her in a quiet area. Limit noise and unnecessary visitors and feed her as much of her regular, nutritionally complete diet as she wants to eat. You can supplement her diet, if your veterinarian advises it.

Remember that she will look pretty shopworn with an almost certain loss of coat during her puppy production. You will be interested in her puppies, to be sure, but be gentle and reassuring with her, especially with the first litter. Give her praise and don't just ooh-and-ah over her puppies.

Weaning

Weaning the puppies can begin anywhere from four to six weeks after birth. You can assist your Pom mother by moistening some premium-quality puppy food and getting the puppies interested in their new food form. Let them taste the food on your fingers and gradually introduce them to it under controlled circumstances.

Puppy Socialization

You must now fill the position of assistant socializer of the puppies. You have followed the veterinarian's advice so mother and puppies are all healthy. You and the mother dog have seen the puppies through their early growth stages, from the time when they were blind and helpless, completely dependent on you and her. You have watched them grow, open their eyes, take clumsy steps, and identify you as their friend. You have handled them on a regular basis and have done so gently. They are now active little balls of fur competing for care and attention. They will have their own pecking order, even in a small litter. You will have learned much about canine behavior by watching their actions. You have supplied the puppies with lots of human contact, kept them in a safe environment, and helped them learn the first lessons that will bring them full circle to the time when they, like the puppy you chose at the start of this adventure, are ready to learn how to be responsible adult Pomeranians.

Your responsibilities now are similar to those you had when you brought your puppy home. You must see that the puppies are safe and comfortable. You should have some good help in this from the mother dog. She will have given them some valuable early lessons in what is expected of them.

You are now in the reverse position of when you were seeking a Pom puppy. You now have puppies that will need loving, responsible care and you will face the quandary that so many breeders experience: "Now that we've got them, what do we do with them?" Remember that you are responsible for these puppies being alive and that while they are alive, the responsibility for their ultimate well-being is yours.

MEDICAL CARE

Maintaining Health

Preventing health problems is far less costly, and far less painful, than treating health problems. By creating a healthy environment and by having a preventive orientation, you can accomplish much in the way of keeping your Pom safe from injuries, diseases, and other unhealthy conditions. You already know about the possible health hazards posed by small children and big dogs; you already know about puppy-proofing your home; you already know about the potential bone breaking that can come from even moderate jumping, falls, or misdirected human feet. Now here is some additional information you can add to your stock of knowledge. Armed with the ways to stop problems before they occur, you are on your way to keeping your Pom as healthy as possible for as long at it lives.

Medical Care Team

Your Pomeranian will need to have a team of concerned humans to make its good health the rule rather than the exception. This team will consist of you, the other members of your household, your Pom's groomer, and foremost, your Pom's veterinarian.

After a Pomeranian's family, the closest friend the dog should have is its veterinarian. Only through regular exams and veterinary care can your Pomeranian be healthy and happy and live a full life.

You and your family have already learned some accident-prevention ideas. Now you need to learn about the most common diseases, parasites, and medical conditions that may confront your dog, and how to recognize these health enemies.

As previously mentioned, your Pom's groomer is in an excellent position to monitor several aspects of your dog's health. Not only does a skilled, professional groomer bring a good deal of expertise and experience to your team, he or she also sees your dog often enough to know a lot about it and rarely enough to notice any subtle changes that may be too gradual to be easily spotted by you and your family, who see the Pomeranian every day. Make it a point to let the groomer know that his or her opinion is respected and welcome in matters concerning the health of your Pom.

The Veterinarian

The key member of this health team is, of course, your veterinarian. Nobody is better trained or more knowledgeable about how to keep your Pomeranian healthy than your dog's veterinarian. The best use of a veterinarian is not only in an emergency, but as a caring professional who sees your pet on regular visits. Take time to establish a good rapport with this key team member. The veterinarian's skill and knowledge will be vital from your dog's puppyhood to its old age.

Strive for good, clear communication with your Pom's veterinarian. He or she will need to know accurate information, without embellishment, to make the proper diagnosis and prescribe an effective treatment. Ask questions and make sure you understand the answers. Neither you nor the veterinarian can really help your Pomeranian with partial or inaccurate knowledge.

Find a good veterinarian and then follow his or her instructions—*to the letter.* You may have a great deal of knowledge about a great many things, but trust the medical care of your pet to the person with the best training—your veterinarian.

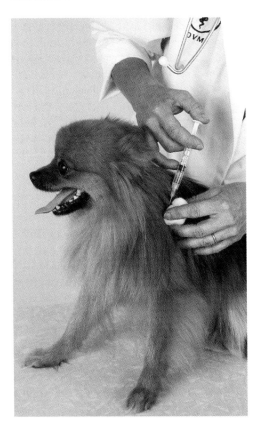

Preventive Care

Your in-home health care and routine visits to the veterinarian provide the basis for continuing good health for your Pomeranian, but the best veterinarian in the world can't help your dog if you don't take it to the veterinarian's office on a regular schedule.

This schedule will include visits for checkups and for vaccinations. Checkups will spot many potential health problems before they arise; vaccinations will protect your Pomeranian from a number of diseases and infections. Having your Pom immunized against a number of diseases isn't just smart; in some places, it's the law.

Vaccinations

Your puppy should have received its first immunizations while still under the breeder's care. The first shots include initial vaccinations for distemper, parvovirus, hepatitis, leptospirosis, parainfluenza, coronavirus, and bordetella. At six weeks of age, your puppy should have gotten these shots. Follow-up shots will be necessary for most of these immunizations and your veterinarian will set up a schedule. They are usually needed at 12 weeks and again at 16 weeks. Some diseases require annual booster shots.

Diseases Controlled by Vaccinations

Be sure your veterinarian has a complete record of all vaccinations and other treatments your puppy received before you got it. This is the beginning of your Pom's health record,

Preventive health care begins with immunizations (and regular follow-ups) to keep a pet safe from a number of canine diseases.

which should be kept up to date as long as the dog lives.

Canine Distemper (CD): Once the most deadly killer of puppies and young dogs, distemper is a disease that is both widespread and highly contagious. Distemper affects all the members of the canine family and a number of other small mammals. It was not uncommon, a number of years ago, for distemper to rage through a kennel and destroy most of the young dogs and all of the puppies.

As a viral disease, the onset of symptoms would rapidly appear about a week after exposure to an infected animal. At first, distemper would resemble a cold with a fever and a runny nose. The dog would then typically stop eating and appear tired and listless. Sometimes, vomiting or diarrhea would be present and the skin leathers of the nose and pads of the feet would thicken, which prompted old time dog breeders to label distemper as "hard pad disease."

Although some dogs would seem to recover, distemper would linger and later reappear in the form of convulsions, nervous twitching, paralysis, and eventually, death. Thankfully, vaccination has greatly decreased the incidence of this dreadful disease.

Rabies: As your Pomeranian grows up, it will need a rabies vaccination. It will also require periodic rabies booster shots throughout its life. Rabies or hydrophobia was the feared "madness" that occurred periodically since earliest time among dogs and other animals. The mere mention of the word can still conjure up terrible mental pictures of mad dogs, foaming at the mouth and running amok terrorizing a neighborhood.

Rabies is an acute infectious disease of warm-blooded mammals, including man, transmitted most commonly by a bite. Skunks, raccoons, bats, and foxes are among the wild animals thought to be the most common carriers of rabies. The disease still affects populations of wild animals in some parts of the world, but has been effectively eradicated in England and other countries largely by the use of strict quarantine.

Because of the fatal nature of the disease, its frightening symptoms, and the relative ease of transmission in earlier times, rabies joined the bubonic plague, leprosy, anthrax, and a few other so-called nightmare diseases that have been largely eradicated, thanks to advances in medicine. Louis Pasteur in 1885 developed the first vaccine against rabies. His early work, crude by modern standards, set the stage for a number of other immunizations that have made rabies a rare disease among humans—about one case a year occurs in the United States—but a disease that every dog should be vaccinated against.

Leptospirosis: Leptospirosis is another canine disease that can be transmitted by humans. This bacterial disease is most commonly spread by exposure to an animal with leptospirosis or by ingestion of water that has been polluted by the urine of an infected animal.

You can recognize leptospirosis by a loss of appetite, fever, vomiting, and diarrhea. In advanced cases, serious damage to the liver and kidneys can result. Jaundice, weak hindquarters, sores in the soft tissue in the mouth, and abdominal pain are also symptoms that dogs infected with leptospirosis might evidence.

Parvovirus: The parvovirus attacks the intestines of dogs. It causes a viral infection than can result in death for many unvaccinated or untreated dogs at any time, but especially affects puppies under four months of age.

Being outside exposes your Pom to a number of potential medical problems ranging from accidents to parasites. Always carefully go over your pet after it has spent some time outside.

Listlessness and loss of appetite, followed by vomiting as well as heavy, sometimes bloody diarrhea, are classic parvovirus symptoms. Infected puppies will suffer from extreme dehydration. Unless the dog receives prompt veterinary care, death will often be the outcome. If medical care is given to offset the effects of the dehydration and to handle any secondary infections, there is a reasonable chance of survival.

Parvovirus can be controlled by vaccination and common sense. Any unvaccinated dog should be viewed as a potential victim. If your Pom is not vaccinated and should encounter a dog infected with parvovirus on the street during your walks, you could be inviting this dangerous virus to attack your dog.

Hepatitis: Now known as CAV-1 (Canine Adenovirus, Type 1), infectious canine hepatitis can affect a dog of any age. The severity of the disease can range from a relatively light ailment to a death-dealing viral infection that can cause some dogs to die in less than a day after the symptoms first appear.

The symptoms of this disease are listlessness, fever, tonsillitis, abdominal pain, vomiting, and hemorrhaging.

Parainfluenza: Commonly called kennel cough, parainfluenza is a highly contagious viral disease. It can spread quickly through dogs that are kept near one another, as in a kennel, but is certainly not limited to kennels. Parainfluenza brings on tracheobronchitis, which is characterized by a dry, hacking cough followed by retching to expel throat mucus.

Parainfluenza, in and of itself, is not that debilitating. Untreated, however, this so-called "kennel cough" can leave a dog very susceptible to more severe respiratory ailments and secondary infections. As with the other preventable diseases, parainfluenza should be prevented by vaccination. Good treatment for tracheobronchitis is best provided by a veterinarian with the patient kept away from other dogs to lessen the contagion.

Coronavirus: Coronavirus is another highly contagious disease that affects unvaccinated dogs of all ages. Coronavirus looks very much like parvovirus. Your veterinarian will be able to distinguish one from the other.

Typically, coronavirus causes severe diarrhea, often foul smelling, watery, and sometimes marked with blood. Regardless of the final diagnosis, parvovirus or coronavirus, if your Pom has such symptoms, call your veterinarian and isolate the dog until you can take it to the animal hospital.

Bordetella: Bordetella, a companion disease to parainfluenza (kennel cough), is a bacterial infection often connected with tracheobronchitis. Your veterinarian will be able to prevent bordetella by an immunization that will strike at the whole range of the tracheobronchial infections.

Parasites

Internal Parasites

Worms are common in adult dogs and puppies, and can pose serious health problems. Your veterinarian can find out if worms are present in your Pomeranian and will prescribe the most appropriate treatment.

Worms are generally detected by microscopic examination of fecal material or of a blood sample. The most common worms infecting dogs are roundworms, hookworms, tapeworms, heartworms, and whipworms. Each of these must be dealt with by a specific treatment from your veterinarian.

Roundworms: Roundworms are most often found in puppies, although dogs of any age can be infested. Puppies generally get roundworms even before they are born if the mother dog has them.

Puppies that have roundworms will not thrive. Their appearance is often just not quite as sharp and shiny as

uninfected puppies. They may have a pendulous abdomen (potbelly). They may also pass worms through their stools or when they vomit. Your veterinarian can handle the medical aspects of eliminating roundworms after making a stool examination first and an evaluation of the dog later.

Good housekeeping on your part will help eliminate these parasites. Keep the puppies' area extremely clean and sanitized, and safely dispose of any and all stools promptly.

Hookworms: Although hookworms will infect dogs of all ages, these bloodsuckers will really cause your puppies to do poorly. The puppies have bloody or inky stools, fail to maintain weight, and fail to eat properly. Since hookworms attach themselves to the small intestine and suck blood, anemia can be the sometimes fatal result.

The flea, which plays a key role in the life cycle of the tapeworm, actually serves as an intermediate host for the tapeworm's eggs. When a dog swallows an infested flea, the eggs mature in the dog's intestines. Tapeworm eggs can also be found in raw meat and fish.

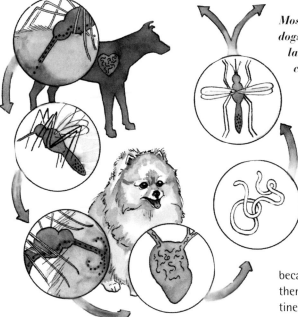

Mosquitoes spread heartworm from infected dogs to uninfected dogs. The heartworm larvae mature in the dog's heart and cause great damage there.

Just because your Pomeranian is predominantly an inside dog, don't ignore the preventive treatment that can keep this parasite from clogging your dog's heart. Your veterinarian can help you with medication that will prevent infestation. This medication will prevent the need for an expensive, possibly risky, and prolonged treatment and save your pet from an early and miserable death.

Whipworms: Whipworms, so named because of their threadlike appearance, attach themselves to the walls of a dog's large intestine. Here they feed and lay their eggs, which are spread through the feces; another animal comes along and eats the whipworm eggs, and the whole cycle starts over again.

In mild cases, whipworms can be hard to detect. In severe instances, as the worms grow, dogs become anemic, lose weight, and are plagued by diarrhea. Heavy infestations in a dog's yard or kennel area require an increase in visits to the veterinarian.

External Parasites

Fleas: Fleas are the bane of many a dog's existence. They are the most common external parasite afflicting dogs. They feed on your dog's blood and in extreme cases cause anemia. Generally, they can make your Pomeranian miserable, and, since many Poms live inside, fleas can make dog owners miserable too. Your dog can even become infected with tapeworms transmitted by fleas.

See your veterinarian promptly and keep your dogs away from infested areas; as with roundworms, dispose of all stools as soon as possible.

Tapeworms: Tapeworms are commonly transmitted by fleas. Although they rarely debilitate a dog, these flat, segmented parasites rob your dog of its health.

Your veterinarian can treat the dog and assist you in a plan to prevent the tapeworm's return. This parasite is just another good reason for eliminating fleas from your dog's environment (see discussion of fleas that follows).

Heartworms: This wide-ranging worm is transmitted to dogs by a mosquito. The mosquito, itself infested with the heartworm larvae, passes these larvae into a dog's bloodstream and ultimately to its heart.

Some Pomeranians suffer from flea bite allergy. While fleas are bothersome to all dogs, dogs that are allergic to fleas suffer much more. Hair loss, skin problems, and incessant scratching may indicate this allergy. Prompt treatment by a veterinarian can do much to alleviate this uncomfortable condition.

Flea bite allergy is also another good reason for working diligently to eliminate fleas from your Pom's environment and to keep them out. Dealing with fleas involves a warfare mentality—a them-or-us kind of thinking. You have to hit fleas at *every* possible site in order to achieve even limited victory. Everywhere an infested dog has been will harbor fleas—the bed, the yard, the doghouse, the car, your house. If you fail to attack the fleas in *any* of these areas, then you have failed—they will be back.

Flea dips, flea shampoos, flea powder, flea collars, and flea sprays are all designed for use on the dog. Be sure to treat the Pom's "den" and its bedding. Flea foggers will provide some relief for your home. In severe cases you may need to call an exterminator. Fleas spend only about 10 percent of their time on the dog, which means that 90 percent of the time fleas are available to visit your home, yard, and so on.

There are a number of new flea-repellent products available from your veterinarian, including new tablets that can be given orally. There are also liquid products that are applied topically on the dog's skin once a month. New developments in flea collars have appeared that keep fleas off your dog rather than killing the fleas once they arrive. Some of these new products kill flea eggs; others target only adult fleas. Your veterinarian can advise you about these new flea fighters.

Regular monthly grooming by a professional will spot fleas before they get to the severe stage. But always remember you cannot beat a flea infestation by dealing with just part of the problem. The *entire* environment must be treated.

Ticks: On walks or while playing outside, your Pomeranian can come in contact with another vicious bloodsucker, the tick. Although regular dips will control ticks rather well, you need to know how to handle them if you see them.

This Pomeranian mother is especially watchful over her puppy. As an owner, you also need to be observant about your Pom's health.

Ticks are much larger than fleas, and as they engorge on blood, they can get as big as a marble if left in place. Never simply pull a tick off your dog. You will leave part of its mouth parts in the dog, which may cause infection. To get them out cleanly:

✔ Place a drop of alcohol at the location where the tick is attached to the skin. Let the alcohol cause the tick to loosen its grip a bit.

✔ Using tweezers, grasp the tick as close to the dog's skin as possible and pull slowly. Be sure to get the mouth of the tick when you pull the pest away.

✔ Put alcohol on the bite and dispose of the tick carefully, as it can get back on the dog or on you if simply dropped on the ground.

Ticks have gained recent notoriety with the discovery of Lyme disease in humans. This potentially life-threatening disease is transmitted by the deer tick and has been found in many areas across the United States. If a tick bites you, save it and see a medical professional immediately to identify it.

Ear mites: One parasite that can cause your Pomeranian great discomfort is the ear mite. These microscopic mites live in the ear canal. They cause the development of a dark waxy residue and can be easily transmitted to and from other dogs (or cats). Symptoms include head shaking and ear scratching. The veterinarian can identify and treat mites quickly and effectively.

Mange: Another problem brought to the dog by mites is mange. There are two kinds: red mange (demodectic) and scabies (sarcoptic).

Red mange especially affects old dogs and young puppies and causes scruffy hair loss and other symptoms. It varies in degree of severity from dog to dog. Itching may sometimes accompany red mange. Seek help immediately; don't mess around with mange.

Scabies mites burrow into the dog's epidermal skin layer. They are highly contagious and can spread from your dog to other dogs or to you. Sarcoptic mange causes unsightly hair loss and a lot of itching.

Your groomer may act as an early warning system here. See your veterinarian immediately for proper diagnosis and treatment.

Other skin problems: Like other dog breeds, Pomeranians are sometimes beset with any of a number of skin problems—allergies, fungi, and

The veterinarian is examining this puppy's ears. The ears of a Pomeranian can house a myriad of problems from infections to parasites. At home, Pom owners should also regularly monitor the condition of their dog's ears.

The large and prominent eyes of the Pomeranian make them the focal point of every veterinary visit. Eye care should be both preventive and treatment-oriented, with a pet's owner paying close attention to the Pom's eyes on a daily basis.

so on. Flea bite allergy is one skin problem that stems directly from an allergic reaction to fleas (see page 71). Some dogs may develop allergies to certain foods or to some aspect of their environment. Your veterinarian can usually pinpoint the sources of these conditions and help it by either preventing the problem or dealing with it.

It is important to recognize that some skin conditions may be of a genetic origin. Your dog's problem may be something that it inherited from its parents, just another good reason to take special care in choosing a Pomeranian puppy. Rely on your veterinarian in diagnosing and treating skin problems. Home remedies here can often make a condition much worse. Let a professional, with all the information and resources available, develop the treatment plan for your Pomeranian. You won't regret it—nor will your pet.

Common Health Problems

Vomiting and Diarrhea

Some vomiting and diarrhea can result from normal factors, such as dietetic changes, or from stress, but in puppies these problems are most commonly caused by intestinal parasites. Both vomiting and diarrhea are possible indicators of other, more serious conditions. Any prolonged

vomiting or diarrhea that your Pom experiences deserves at least a call to the veterinarian's office for advice. Early treatment is effective treatment. Until you have gained more experience, take care in all such situations.

If either vomiting or diarrhea becomes severe or continues for more than 12 to 24 hours, you would be wise to take your Pom to your veterinarian.

Constipation

If your Pom has not been experiencing normal bowel movements, or if the dog is clearly straining to defecate, constipation may be the cause. Many dietetic causes, such as eating bones or a sudden change in dog food, can cause constipation. Sometimes a Pom that has been traveling and has not been allowed relief walks on a regular basis will become constipated.

Most constipation is a minor problem, but check with your veterinarian if it continues, especially if the dog is in obvious pain and crying out while trying to defecate.

Impacted Anal Glands

The anal glands lie just under the skin on each side of the anus. Normally these glands are emptied of their strong-smelling secretions during defecation. Sometimes, however, these glands become clogged (impacted) and must be emptied by hand. Some groomers will provide this service. Your veterinarian can also show you how to do this. When you see a Pomeranian scooting along the floor or ground, dragging its rear end, impacted anal glands or possible tapeworm irritation could be the cause.

Regular veterinary examinations, starting early in your Pom's life, will prevent many problems and help in quick healing with many others. Budget the cost of such ongoing care when you consider obtaining a Pomeranian puppy.

Special Health Concerns

Patellar Luxation

A luxated patella, in more common terms, is a dislocated kneecap. This condition, usually considered inherited, is common to several toy breeds, including the Pomeranian. Luxating patellas can vary with degree of severity, from cases requiring surgery to barely noticeable conditions. Veterinarians will help devise appropriate treatment modalities for each individual occurrence of this problem. Dogs with luxating patellas should not be bred regardless of the degree of severity.

Collapsing Trachea

This birth defect, often seen in toy breed dogs, causes coughing and labored breathing. As with all other health matters affecting your Pomeranian, your veterinarian is your best source for information about this defect.

Anesthetic Reaction

Many toy breeds, including the Pomeranian, can have serious tolerance problems to anesthetics. Some newer anesthetics, such as Isoflourine, seem to have no contraindications for Pomeranians. Most veterinarians know about this problem of toy breeds and reactions have been greatly reduced.

Hypoplasia of Dens

This condition, thought to be of an inherited nature, has been reported in Pomeranians. It results in atlanto-axial subluxation, which is partial dislocation of the first and second cervical vertebras. Hypoplasia of dens (also referred to as odontoid process) can be seen at any age. It may produce neck pain, and sometimes paralysis can result.

Other Inherited Problems

As with many breeds, especially toy breeds, there are a number of other conditions that may be inherited; some families or strains of Poms have them more often than others. For example, Poms with extreme dwarfism, as seen in "teacup" Poms, tend to have more inherited health problems than regular Poms. Consult with Pomeranian experts about the problems observed, however rarely, in their breeding lines.

Emergency Care

Poisoning

Protecting your Pom puppy from some toxic products and conditions has been discussed (see Checklist, page 36). There are other accidental poisoning possibilities you should know about that will generally require immediate veterinary care:

✔ Antifreeze is highly poisonous but has an odor and taste that attract dogs.

Medicines prescribed by a skillful veterinarian are only good if they are correctly given after the Pomeranian gets back home. This pet owner is giving a Pom a pill hidden in a dollop of peanut butter.

✔ A number of indoor and yard plants are deadly if eaten.

✔ Chocolate can be poisonous to most dogs.

✔ Some insect bites or stings can cause strong allergic reactions in your Pomeranian.

Be alert to listlessness, convulsions, disoriented behavior, vomiting, diarrhea, and a change in the color of mucous membranes. Get your pet to the veterinarian as soon as possible when these symptoms appear.

Accidents

Many accidents can be prevented by just thinking ahead and being a little creatively paranoid about things that can hurt your Pom. However, as careful as you are, accidents still happen.

If your Pomeranian has been injured, be careful not to make the injury worse or to be bitten by a dog in pain. Using a small piece of cloth, a shoestring, or a handkerchief as a muzzle, gently lift your Pom and place it on a makeshift stretcher made of your shirt, a towel, or some other cloth that will allow you to move the injured dog without danger of further injury. Call your veterinarian's office to alert the staff to the situation and transport your dog there.

Bleeding

If your Pomeranian appears to be bleeding, identify the source of the blood and apply firm but gentle pressure to the area. If the injury is

Bright eyes, full coats, and mischievous looks typify the healthy Pomeranian.

on an extremity, place a tourniquet between the wound and the heart, but be sure to loosen it every 15 minutes. Continued bleeding or any significant blood loss, or a gaping wound will require veterinary attention. Treat any bleeding as a serious condition.

Heatstroke

A healthy, happy Pomeranian can be dying or dead in just a few minutes in a car with poor ventilation and high inside temperature. The double coat of the Pomeranian cannot insulate the dog in a closed space. Because Poms love to travel, they are often subjected to this danger, one that is frequently ignored even by caring Pomeranian owners. Just a few minutes in the sun, even on a moderately warm day—60°F (15.6°C) or so—or even with some windows partially rolled down can lead to the death of the dog.

One Pom fancier was returning from a trip to the groomer when he was stopped by the police for a minor traffic violation. He was asked to step away from the car and approach the police car to get his ticket, have his license checked, and so forth. In just that short time, the Pom began to show heatstroke symptoms. Thanks to the police, now in an escort role, the dog was rushed to the veterinarian and its life was saved. *Never, never* take chances by leaving your Pom in an enclosed area unattended. It is fatal to a little longhaired dog.

Heatstroke symptoms include a dazed look and rapid, shallow panting with a high fever. The dog's gums will be bright red. This is one situation where you must act before going to the veterinarian. Immediately lower the dog's temperature with cool water or with a mixture of cool water and alcohol. Rush it to the *nearest* veterinary hospital immediately.

Old Age

Aging is a natural process that will affect both you and your Pomeranian. The bouncy puppy will give way to the young adult, which will become the mature dog, which will become your long-time companion and old friend. Pomeranians normally have a long life span, but aging is not without its adjustments. As your Pomeranian begins to reach eight or nine years of age—some dogs age more quickly than others—certain changes will become evident. Your Pom may begin to slow down a little, sleep more, and generally be less active.

Your Pom may begin to experience certain age-related problems with its teeth and gums, bowels and bladder, eyesight, and hearing. Your good preventive care that began in puppyhood, along with regular veterinarian visits, can forestall or delay many of these concerns, but if your Pom lives long enough, some age-related troubles will present themselves.

Euthanasia

When in the natural course of your Pom's life, age, infirmity, or terminal illness makes that life a painful, negative experience for your Pomeranian, you have a difficult decision to make. It is never easy to say good-bye to a loving pet whose life has made yours so much brighter just by being there. It will be even harder to see that same loving pet in constant pain as it goes about even basic daily activities.

Discuss this with your veterinarian, who has taken care of your dog for a long time and personally cares about it too. Euthanasia, although a painful decision for you, is painless and humane for your old friend. It should be considered when your Pomeranian can no longer experience even the simply joy of being because it is enduring a life of increasing discomfort, disability, and suffering.

Teeth

Throughout the life of your Pomeranian, tartar buildup on its teeth will be a problem. Feeding a premium-quality dry dog food will serve as an abrasive to help keep your Pom's teeth clean. Chew toys, nylon bones, and similar products will also help, but as with humans, brushing from puppyhood on will help keep down plaque and tartar. If you pay attention to your Pom's teeth early in its life and consistently thereafter, your dog will have healthier teeth and fresher breath.

If you use one of the new canine oral care kits, which contain a special toothbrush and veterinary dentifrice, on a regular basis, your Pom will have a much better chance to avoid dental problems later on. Weak, loose, or decayed teeth and gum problems can plague older Pomeranians and cause other health problems. You could have your veterinarian begin to clean your pup's teeth early in its life. He or she can do full and thorough teeth cleaning, which may require general anesthesia. Remember, regular preventive care can greatly eliminate most canine dental problems.

Eyes

The Pomeranian's eyes are large and prominent. Eye care, under normal conditions, is not a major problem. Always use good preventive measures such as avoiding any sharp objects at eye level that might harm your Pomeranian.

Through regular inspections for tartar and plaque buildup, and good dental care, you can help your Pomeranian avoid many tooth problems.

Angry cats have already been mentioned for their danger potential (see page 24).

You may, on occasion, see some mucouslike matter collecting in the corners of your dog's eyes. This is of no real consequence. Simply use a tissue and gently wipe the material out of the eyes.

As with other medical matters, use common sense. If your Pom begins to have excessive eye discharge, redness, or evident discomfort, consult your veterinarian. As with humans, Pomeranians can suffer from exposure to chemical fumes, such as those from household cleaners, exterminating products, and so forth, or to smoke from a cigarette or a fireplace. Just a little awareness of what life is like at its level of under 12 inches (30 cm) will help you protect your Pom's eyes.

Cataracts: Older dogs, including older Pomeranians, sometimes develop cataracts, a thick opaqueness of or involving the lens. In this case, you will notice a gradual "clouding" of the eye. Cataracts can be part of the aging process. Other than the cosmetic aspects and some vision impairment, cataracts are not usually serious.

Trimming your Pomeranian's nails is not difficult. Ask your groomer or veterinarian to show you how to do it. Remember, if you cut the nails yourself, trim only the outer points. Avoid cutting into the quick.

Ears

Much of the regular observation you do to guard against ear mites (see page 72) will help you monitor overall ear health. Your groomer and your veterinarian will also help you prevent problems here. If the ears begin to show inflammation or the dog is obviously repeatedly bothered by its ears, there may be an infection. Don't delay in seeking professional care.

If your Pom has access to a wooded area, you need to know that the ears are a favorite target area for ticks. Always check for these critters if your Pom has been where ticks may be lurking (see page 71).

Nails

Part of the consistent care regimen for your Pomeranian will be regular attention to its toenails. Beginning while your Pom is still a puppy, its nails should be kept trimmed. By starting early and gently, your Pom will not fear nail trimming, which it will need on a monthly basis for the rest of its life. Failure to keep the nails at an appropriate length can result in painful lameness for Poms, whose way of walking depends on them being up on their tiptoes.

Your groomer can handle the nail trimming during the monthly grooming session, but you can trim the nails yourself with a good pair of clippers and keep them neat with a good nail file. Get your groomer or veterinarian to show you how to use them. Practice on round toothpicks to learn to cut off just the tip of the nail; you must avoid the "quick" or center of the nail, which will bleed if it is cut. You can use

styptic powder if you do accidentally cut the nail too short.

Administering Medicine

While much of your Pom's health care will rest in the hands of your veterinarian, being able to administer prescription medicines is important. Your Pomeranian may not like taking medicine and may spit out pills and capsules. One way to get pills, such as monthly heartworm medication, into the Pom is by hiding them in some treat item, such as on a small piece of bread smeared with smooth peanut butter.

The direct approach is to simply open your Pom's mouth, tilting the head back just a little way and placing the pill as far back on the tongue as you can. Close the dog's mouth and wait for it to swallow. *It is important not to just casually toss the pill into the dog's mouth or tilt the head back too far; the pill could be caught in the windpipe instead of going down the throat.* Liquid medicine is administered in a similar way by tilting the head back only slightly and pouring the liquid dosage into the back of the dog's mouth. Tilting the head too far back can also cause possible choking as the liquid may flow into the windpipe.

TRAINING YOUR POMERANIAN

Pack Behavior

Your cute, cuddly Pomeranian puppy is a pack animal just like the wolf, the sled dog, or the foxhound. Pack behavior is a natural, integral part of your puppy and the key to teaching it to be a well-trained, good canine citizen.

The pack, in simple terms, is a canine caste system where each member has and knows its place. The pack provides security and a sense of belonging that is crucial to a well-adjusted dog. Positioning in the pack hierarchy is usually based on physical strength and experience. Within it the strongest and most savvy male fills the role of "alpha" or first male.

The alpha dog leads the pack. He adjudicates differences between pack members, enforces his will on the pack, and helps train the young or inexperienced in what is expected of them as pack members. He remains the alpha dog as long as he is the strongest. You will have to perform this role for your Pomeranian and your family will have to serve as the pack members. Your puppy will have already been taught pack behavior by its mother and littermates. You and the other members of your household will

Pomeranians need to become full members of the family. The family then constitutes the Pom's pack, an important social element in every dog's life and a key element in dog training.

be a logical and necessary extension of what the mother dog began.

Training will be much more easily accomplished if you follow the example of your Pom's mother. She taught the puppy, almost from the moment of its birth, lessons it would need to survive. As the pup grew, she reprimanded it, loved it, and instructed it in a pattern that you can and should follow:

1. She admonished the puppy *quickly* for any misdeeds, while the puppy, with its short attention span, could identify action with outcome.

2. She corrected the puppy *fairly*, neither overreacting nor underreacting to its misdeed.

3. She was *consistent* in her treatment of the puppy. A particular behavior did not get a loving lick one time and a warning growl the next.

4. She went about her training *without anger.* She didn't savagely attack the puppy for a misdeed, nor did she bark at it endlessly in an effort to "verbalize" the puppy into correct behavior.

5. She showed that she *loved* the puppy and made it feel secure, even if it had done something that had warranted correction earlier in the day. She didn't withhold love to force the puppy to act correctly.

There is much to learn from the lessons taught by the mother. Not only does your puppy already understand these lessons, but the lessons worked for her and will work for you.

When you take your Pom from its mother and the security of the litter-pack, you should immediately move to fill this gap. You and your family would do well to understand the role of the pack in the emotional well-being of your Pomeranian. You, or your designated person, must become the alpha dog to help this youngster learn its lessons. Your Pomeranian will want to please you after it knows that you love it and will care for it. How your Pom goes about learning what it must do to please you is up to you. The puppy won't learn these lessons by simple osmosis; it must be trained.

When to Begin

Some lessons, such as housebreaking and basic rules, can begin immediately. More involved training should begin between five and eight months, based on your dog's own timetable. Some pups are ready earlier than others. Don't push your puppy to be an "early bloomer." Let the pup learn what it can in the security of the home, and when it seems ready—physically and mentally mature—for further training, move on to the next step. Always remember the mother dog's training example:

1. Be quick to reprimand.

2. Be fair.

3. Be consistent.

4. Do not display anger.

5. Create an environment where affection and security are clearly evident.

Training Essentials

1. You and your puppy will need a regularly set time—perhaps a couple of times a day—free from distractions such as other dogs, running children, and so forth. This time should be short, not more than 15 minutes, and while enjoyable, it should be worktime not playtime.

2. You need to have a clear idea—perhaps discussed with other members of your family—of what you want your Pomeranian to learn. Consistency is important. You can't be correcting behavior that everyone else in the family ignores or even rewards.

3. You are the boss, the alpha dog. Use a stern tone of voice during the training sessions to differentiate from other times when you and the Pom are together. This is an authoritarian hat, but not a drill sergeant's hat. These sessions should never be conducted when you are angry at the dog, your spouse, or your boss.

4. Each session should be conducted as a class. Learning is the objective. If the command *"Come"* is to be taught today, don't try to get into the variations of *"Fetch"* or *"Roll over."* Stay to the subject. Review previous lessons and praise the dog when it does something right. Correct *each* time it doesn't do what it should, but make sure that the dog understands the desired action. If you can't get a lesson across, go back to something the dog does well. Do that several times, then praise the dog and stop for the day.

5. Use appropriate praise for a successfully learned behavior. This doesn't mean the dog does what you want one time and then you roughhouse for the rest of the time. Praise effectively, but save play for later, allowing a few minutes of lag time between the lesson and playtime so that the two are not confused.

6. Correct misdeeds immediately while you can so that the puppy can identify the action or misdeed with your reprimand. Don't attempt to punish the dog for something it has done

Pomeranians make excellent pets. Young people, properly supervised, can learn a great deal about responsibility by having a pet Pomeranian.

some time ago. It won't remember or understand why you are reprimanding; free-floating reprimands don't do anything but confuse the dog when you do want to change its behavior.

7. Be patient and never lose your temper. Ranting and raving or whipping the dog can ruin the puppy's trust in you. Remember the lack of anger the mother dog used with the puppies.

Discipline

As mentioned previously, your Pomeranian should never be the victim of severe physical punishment. If you follow the previous train-

ing-session design, a stern voice using the word *"No"* in a firm manner will convey your displeasure.

Some dogs will test the limits of your control and your ability to be the alpha dog; just because a Pom is small doesn't mean this testing won't take place. Counter any such behavior immediately and consistently. You are the alpha dog and as such you can't put up with such behavior.

Setting the Stage

Your puppy will need to learn its name early in your relationship. If your dog is a registered Pom from a long line of champions, it may have an impressive or even pretentious formal name. It is amazing how a tiny puppy that just fits in your hand could have a moniker such as "Mandrake's Lothar of Hambletonian." It will

Responsible pet owners always have their pets under some form of control: a leash, a fenced yard, or properly trained. Just because a Pomeranian is a small dog doesn't mean that it wouldn't benefit from (and enjoy) dog training classes.

canine interaction—the ability of the human to find a way to communicate with the canine and shape the canine's behavior, having a good time in the process.

Collar and Leash

A chain or nylon training collar of the type commonly called a "choke chain" is the most effective and humane way to train your Pom. When you use the collar correctly, the collar does not choke the dog; it merely provides restraining, correcting pressure when given a quick tug upward. This gets the pup's attention and also serves as a correcting method. The quick tug and the stern word *"No"* let the puppy know it has done wrong. The collar will need to be large enough to go over your Pom's head at its widest part with about one inch to spare but not much more. This collar is generally used for training only. Before beginning the lesson, exchange your Pom's regular collar—the one attached to its personal identification and rabies vaccination tags—for the training collar.

With the training collar you will need a $\frac{1}{2}$- to 1-inch (1.3–2.5 cm) wide leash (or lead) measuring about 6 feet (1.8 m) long. The lead can be leather, web, or nylon. It will need to have a swivel snap at one end for fastening through the ring on the training collar. At the other end, the lead should have a comfortable

need a short name that will be its "call name," preferably of one syllable. Name your puppy and stick with that name. Have your family stick with it. If the dog's call name is Mike, call him Mike, not Mickey or Mikey Poo. Your dog definitely needs to know what its name is in order for training to begin.

Basic Training

When your Pomeranian is about five months old, you can be reasonably sure that it is mature enough to learn the basic obedience commands that will make it a more manageable pet. Unfortunately, some owners of toy breeds fail to give their pets the advantages of training. They seem to feel that their little dog can be carried and therefore be made to do what is required. These people and their pets are missing one of the great joys of human-hand loop. This lead is, of course, longer than your normal walking leash.

You should familiarize your puppy with the training collar and with the lead in a carefully orchestrated way so that the puppy will not come to fear or dislike either the collar or the lead. In a large room where there are no obstacles to snag the lead and frighten the puppy, let your Pom run around with the training collar on and the lead trailing along behind. This will give the puppy the feel of the weight of the collar and lead before training time actually rolls around.

Basic Commands

There are five basic commands: *sit, down, stay, heel,* and *come.* With these five skills firmly in its repertoire, your Pom will be a

Never call your Pomeranian to you for a negative reason because your Pom will associate the reason with the command. Always go to the dog for reprimands or anything not viewed by the dog as positive.

better pet or could even pursue further training in the Obedience ring if it has the aptitude and you are so inclined. Be sure to issue clear, one-word commands to your dog, such as *"Sit."* Use the dog's name before each command and be authoritarian in your tone: *"Fluffy, sit!"* Use the same tone each time. Don't confuse your dog by using two commands at one time, such as *"Sit down."* Also remember the keys to canine learning are wrapped up in four rules:

1. Praise enthusiastically.
2. Correct fairly and immediately.
3. Practice consistent repetition.
4. Don't lose your temper.

Sit

The *sit* is a good command. Your pup already knows how to sit; all you need to do is teach it when and where to do so.

✔ With the training collar on and attached to the lead, place your Pom on your left side next to your left leg, while holding the lead in your right hand.

✔ In one continuous, gentle motion, pull the pup's head up with the lead as you push its

hindquarters down with your left hand, giving a firm command, *"Sit,"* as you do so.

✔ When the Pom is in the sitting position, lavishly praise it.

Using the concept of consistent repetition, repeat the lesson until your Pom sits down without its rear end being pushed. Remember to keep the same upward pressure on the lead to prevent a *sit* from becoming a belly flop. If the dog shifts in position, use your left hand to move it back to where it belongs. Keep doing this exercise until the Pomeranian associates the word *"Sit"* and your tone with the praise it gets if it sits down. Soon the Pom will sit upon hearing the word alone without the rear-end push or the raised lead. Always use praise liberally. Make the praise and the lesson stick out in your Pom's mind.

Keep your training time brief. Initially, don't leave the young dog in the sitting position long enough to bore it. Gradually increase the time for sitting. Remember, consistent repetition with praise and correction will help your

pup learn. You may have to begin again each time for a while. Your Pom will learn more quickly with several brief, consistent sessions than with one, long, drawn-out session.

Stay

Do not attempt to teach *stay* until your pup is doing well with *sit*. The *stay* is begun from the *sit* and without that foundation, the command cannot be mastered.

✔ To begin your part of the *stay* command, you must place your dog in a regular sitting position on your left. Keep some pressure on the lead in your right hand to keep the Pom's head up.

✔ Giving the clear, authoritative command *"Stay!"* step away from the dog, moving your right foot first. At the same time, bring the palm of your left hand down in front of the Pomeranian's face. Your command, the stepping away, moving the right foot first, and the hand signal must be simultaneous and done exactly the same way in each repetition.

✔ Keep eye contact with your dog and repeat the *stay* command in the same firm tone as before.

Don't really expect long *stays* initially. Praise the puppy for its *stays* whatever their length, but if it moves toward you, take it back to the starting point, make it sit, and start again with consistent repetition. Patience is the rule here. Your dog loves you and wants to come and be with you. If it has trouble with the *stay*, don't wear it down trying; go back to the *sit*, a command that it can do well, and enthusiastically praise the puppy.

Pomeranians may be small enough to pick up and carry, but every dog deserves to be trained.

Each time the pup obeys the *stay* command, praise it. You will be able to gradually move further away and the puppy will eventually get the idea. Introduce the release word *"Okay"* in a cheerful, happy way when you want to let the puppy know that it can now come to you and be praised.

Because of the conflicts the puppy feels—wanting to please you and wanting to be with you—the *stay* is fairly difficult, but with patience and consistency you will see your Pomeranian master it.

Heel

Now that the training collar and lead are part of your dog's experience, you can teach it to *heel,* a most useful command.

✔ Begin *heel* training with your Pomeranian on your left side, its head next to your left foot, in the *sit* position.

✔ Holding the lead in your right hand and leading with your left foot, step forward saying in your firm, authoritative "alpha" voice, *"Heel!"* Use the dog's name to begin the command as in, *"Mike, heel!"*

✔ If your Pom doesn't move out when you do, snap the lead sharply against your leg and repeat the command, walking away as you do. As soon as your Pom catches up with you, praise it but keep moving, using encouraging praise as long as it stays with you in proper position.

✔ When you stop, tell your dog *"Sit!"* As the Pomeranian becomes more experienced in heeling, it will learn to sit on its own when you stop. Don't let your Pom lag behind or run ahead or edge around to face you. The purpose of the *heel* command is not just to walk your dog but to position the dog on your left and teach it to move and stop when you move and stop. The ultimate goal of heeling would be to have the dog accomplish this without the lead.

Don't drag your Pom with you just to cover some distance. Go back to the *sit* and start again. The *heel* command is difficult for some dogs to learn. Continue your use of tugs on the lead to keep your Pom moving and keep its head in line with your left leg. Pomeranians are intelligent and most can pick up heeling in a few consistent, patient lessons.

Down

Down begins with the *sit* and the *stay.*

✔ Using the lead in an opposite movement from the upward pressure used with the *sit* and the *stay,* pull down on the lead with your right hand, presenting the palm of your left hand with a downward motion while clearly giving the command *"Down!"* The small size of the Pom makes this easy to do.

✔ If the dog doesn't want to lie down, put the lead under your left foot and pull up on it, gently forcing the Pom's head downward. Again use the hand signal and the command, *"Down!"*

✔ Once the pup is in the *down* position, heap on the praise. You can help your pup just a bit in the early lessons for this command by using your left hand, as in the *sit* command, but push on the back rather than on the hindquarters. It is the downward direction that this command strives to emphasize, but it should be used in conjunction with the *stay.* The ultimate goal is to cause the Pom to go straight down on its stomach and remain there until released by the *"Okay"* command from you.

The *down* can be a very useful and important command to stop your Pom in its tracks when it might be heading for trouble or danger. Practice the *down* together with *sit* and *stay;* always make sure that your Pomeranian is rewarded when it stays in the *down* position. Using the credo of consistent repetition, you should be able to gradually increase the length of the *down* and even leave the Pom's line of sight and expect it to remain in place. As with the *stay*, your Pom should not move about. Correct it if it does; praise it if it doesn't.

Come

The *come* command may seem simple, but there are several important elements to it. Enthusiasm and use of the dog's name and the command with wide open arms will let your puppy know you really want to be with it. This seems like a natural behavior, yet so many people foolishly call their dogs and then scold, punish, or even whip them. To an intelligent Pomeranian puppy, the command *"Come"* issued by you, or any member of your family, then followed by a reprimand, could cause this natural behavior to be unlearned quickly. *Never* call your dog to you and correct or punish it. If the dog must be corrected, you go to the dog and do it.

✔ Always heap loads of praise on your Pomeranian when it comes at your call. Remember that the dog must learn that *come,* like the other commands, must be obeyed immediately each and every time.

✔ If your dog is a little stubborn or inattentive to the command, give the lead, which of course is still in use, a firm but gentle tug to get movement in your direction started. This method will work, especially when combined with the authoritative command from you as the alpha leader and the warm tones and friendly gesturing that follow it. If not, you can use a little sharper tug with the command.

✔ Have your puppy on a 6-foot (2-m) lead, but a longer lead can be used—up to 20 feet (6 m)—to reinforce the command from a greater distance.

One point in the *come* command differs from the others. This command does not need to be repeated over and over again during a lesson. Use it when you are working on the other lessons or when your dog is involved in play or something else. Always expect the dog to obey this command quickly and praise the dog when it complies.

Remember that saying *"Come"* and then reprimanding is an excellent way to untrain your dog. Teach that point to your family. While discussing this with your family, let each person learn all the different commands and the correct "hows" and "whys" of each part. This will make things much saner for your puppy, because it can't possibly learn when it is getting conflicting usages of the same word from different members of its "pack."

Obedience Classes

If, for whatever reason, you can't seem to teach your Pomeranian—which is unusual—don't hesitate to enlist the help of a professionally run obedience school or class. Another option is a local dog club where obedience lessons are frequently offered. Recognize that much of what will be taught in these classes will be aimed at helping you train yourself to train your dog. There are many other things that a smart Pom can learn beyond the basic commands discussed here. You may want to give your pup or adult dog a chance at higher education.

This Pomeranian is training for an upcoming Agility trial.

Obedience Trials

Obedience trials have become one of the fastest-growing dog-related activities in the United States. If you and your Pomeranian are suited for this activity, you may want to see what Obedience trials are all about.

You can get a copy of the rules from the AKC. This will give you all you need to know about Novice Class competitions. Obedience work isn't for every dog owner or for every dog, but for those who want to learn the various titles (CD, Companion Dog; CDX, Companion Dog Excellent; UD, Utility Dog; OT Ch, Obedience Trial Champion) it can be a wonderful undertaking.

The United Kennel Club (UKC) and the Canadian Kennel Club (CKC) also sanction Obedience trials. Pomeranians are eligible for these trials also.

Barking Behavior

As mentioned earlier, Pomeranians are alert, vocal little dogs that show an interest in everything and everyone. When this interest takes the form of unwarranted barking, some training techniques need to be applied to the problem. Again, the prevention is much better than the cure.

Beginning with the very young puppy on its first night with you, if you let its sad crying cause you to pick it up repeatedly, then you are training that puppy to do something that later you will not like.

Just as you should never encourage begging behavior by feeding tidbits at the dinner table, you can keep yourself from teaching unwarranted barking in much the same way. Simply don't respond to barking when you don't want barking to occur. If your Pom is barking just to get your attention, steel yourself—and teach this to your family—and ignore the dog. Pay attention to it only when there has been no unwarranted barking. It takes time, but if you are patient and consistent, it works.

While housebreaking isn't very hard for most Pomeranians, there are some definite ways to make this key training easier for your pet. Follow these hints to help ease your puppy along the path that leads to its being housebroken:

1. Take your Pom to the "relief spot" after each meal or drink of water.

2. When your Pom relieves itself in the designated area, praise it enthusiastically.

3. Arrange for a relief stop after all long playtimes.

4. Schedule your pup's last relief break as late at night as you possibly can.

5. The very first thing each morning, as early as possible, rush your pup outside.

6. Plan on several relief breaks whenever you and your Pom are home together.

7. Be aware of the warning signs that a puppy, or even an adult dog, displays when it needs to go outside:

✔ Your Pom will have an anxious look on its face.

✔ It will begin circling in one spot, sniffing for the right place to relieve itself.

✔ In an obvious attempt to get your attention, your Pom will whine, whimper, and run toward the door.

✔ Your dog or puppy will begin to squat.

In Case of Accidents

✔ If your puppy can't hold back any longer, pick it up and go calmly (and quickly) to the outside relief spot. *Do this even if your dog has already had an accident.*

✔ Again, wait patiently (and quietly) at the relief spot until your Pom has relieved itself, then heap on the praise, thereby reinforcing the fact that it relieved itself at the right spot.

✔ Thoroughly clean the accident site and apply scent removers that work on enzymes. Do this to each spot to keep from sending false signals about the right place to urinate or defecate.

✔ Do not speak harshly or punish your pup at the relief spot. This should be the place where a puppy knows exactly what to expect; it will relieve itself and get praised for doing so.

✔ As you go with your Pomeranian to the relief spot—and as you wait for action at the site—be quiet. Play is for another time.

✔ *Never rub* your puppy's nose in any urine or defecation. This is an old myth that only results in a confused and soiled puppy.

Never use physical punishment or rub the puppy's nose in any messes it might make. A firm "No" will convey your displeasure, won't scare the puppy, and you won't have to clean up the Pom afterward.

✔ *Never strike* a puppy when it makes a mistake.

✔ Don't scream at a puppy that is not housebroken. You can make some noise, such as clapping your hands, to break an inappropriately defecating or urinating puppy's train of thought. Then hustle the pup outside to the relief spot.

Consistency

Be consistent in all your housebreaking efforts. Make certain that other household members are doing the same things that you are doing and in the same manner.

Note: Never just push a Pomeranian out the door, even into a safe, fenced backyard, to defecate or urinate alone. Your praise is the reward it gets for going in the specific spot each time it goes outside.

Paper Training

If you have to use a paper-training area inside your home, place your pup's food and water as far away from the paper area as possible. Because paper training is less effective, continue to take your Pomeranian outside after meals and drinks and early in the morning and late at night.

Crate Training Hints

✔ Maintain a realistic and positive attitude about the use of crates/cages/carriers and the positive role they can play in providing a "den" for your Pomeranian.

✔ Obtain a large enough crate/cage/carrier to comfortably serve as a den for your Pom when it is an adult. Make a movable, temporary partition to keep the den just the right size as your puppy grows.

✔ Locate such a den in an out-of-the way, but not isolated, place in a part of the household that is always in use but away from any temperature fluctuations that would make it uncomfortable at times.

✔ Put the puppy in the crate/cage/carrier for naps and when it must be left unattended for several hours. Upon your return, immediately take the puppy outside to the relief spot. Praise the puppy when it defecates or urinates and go right back inside with the pup.

✔ Use the stern alpha-leader, authoritative voice to quiet any whining or barking that the pup makes as it is being placed in the makeshift den.

✔ Do not praise the puppy for about ten minutes after it is let out of the crate/cage/carrier. Immediate praise will make getting out more of a reward than you want it to be.

✔ During training, put the puppy back in its den after it has spent about 30 minutes outside of it, and make the puppy quiet down. Through consistent reinforcement, the amount of time you can leave the Pom in the den can be extended.

✔ Don't leave any dog, especially a younger animal, in a crate for an overly long period of time. Your dog won't be able to hold back its need to relieve itself and you will have a real mess to clean up.

✔ Always keep a mat or towel in the den along with a favorite chew toy to make it a comfortable place.

✔ In order to cut down on possible spillage, do not put food or water in the crate/cage/carrier.

✔ Make sure your family and frequent visitors to your house fully understand the importance of crate training and how it must be done.

INFORMATION

Clubs and Organizations

American Pomeranian Club*
Corresponding Secretary
Brenda Turner
3910 Concord Place
Texarkana, TX 75501-2212
Breeder Contact
Jane Lehtinen
(218) 741-2117

American Kennel Club
260 Madison Avenue
New York, NY 10016
(212) 696-8200 (general information)
(212) 696-8246 (AKC library)
www.akc.org

AKC Breeder Referral Hotline
(for the name of a breeder near you)
1-900-407-PUPS (99 cents a minute)

Canadian Kennel Club
89 Skyway Avenue, Suite 100
Etobicoke, Ontario M9W 6R4
Canada
(416) 675-5511
www.ckc.ca

United Kennel Club
100 E. Kilgore Road
Kalamazoo, MI 49001-5598
(616) 343-9020
www.ukcdogs.com

The Kennel Club
1-5 Clarges Street
Picadilly
London W1Y 8AB
England
171-629-5828

American Boarding Kennel Association
4575 Galley Road, Suite 400-A
Colorado Springs, CO 80915

* This address may change as a new officer is
elected. The latest listing can always be
obtained from the American Kennel Club.

Magazines

The AKC Gazette, The Official
Journal for the Sport of Purebred Dogs
American Kennel Club
260 Madison Avenue
New York, NY 10016
www.akc.org

Dog Fancy
Fancy Publications
3 Burroughs
Irvine, CA 92618
(714) 855-8822
www.dogfancy.com

Dog World
Maclean Hunter Publishing Corp.
500 N. Dearborn, Suite 1100
Chicago, IL 60610
www.dogworldmag.com

The Pom Reader
8848 Beverly Hills
Lakeland, FL 33809-1604

The Pomeranian Review
(The official publication of
the American Pomeranian Club)
102 Tudor Lane
Lansing, MI 48906

Pomeranians usually peacefully coexist with other pets in the home.

Books

Coile, D. Caroline. *American Eskimo Dogs.* Hauppauge, NY: Barron's Educational Series, Inc., 1995.

Hughes, Pauline B. *The Pomeranian.* Springfield, MO: Denlinger's Publishers, 1990.

Rice, Dan. *Dogs From A to Z, A Dictionary of Canine Terms.* Hauppauge, NY: Barron's Educational Series, Inc., 1998.

————. *The Complete Book of Dog Breeding.* Hauppauge, NY: Barron's Educational Series, Inc., 1997.

Stahlkuppe, Joe. *Keeshonden.* Hauppauge, NY: Barron's Educational Series, Inc., 1993.

Tietjen, Sari Brewster. *The New Pomeranian.* New York: Howell Book House, 1987.

About the Author

Joe Stahlkuppe is a widely read pet columnist, author, and freelance feature writer. A long-time fan of purebred dogs, he has written several of Barron's Pet Owner's Manuals. He lives on a small farm near Birmingham, Alabama, with his wife, Cathie. He divides his time between his granddaughter, Ann Catherine (who shares his love for pets), and his work as Education and Resource Director for *petsAmerica.com,* a major online pet products and education provider. Joe, a licensed clergyman, is also the host of a long-running talk radio show about pets, *PetsAmericaLIVE.*

Photo Credits

Norvia Behling: pages 2–3, 9, 20, 22, 24, 29, 30, 34, 35, 37, 40, 42–44, 47, 48, 50, 53, 61, 64, 66, 68, 72–75, 80, 83, 93; Tara Darling: pages 8, 12, 85; Kent and Donna Dannen: pages 6, 7, 10, 13, 26, 31, 39, 46, 51, 57, 76, 84, 86, 89, 94; Toni Tucker: pages 4, 11, 32, 54, 71

Cover Photos

Front: Toni Tucker; Back: Norvia Behling; Inside Front: Toni Tucker; Inside Back: Kent and Donna Dannen.

Important Note

This book is concerned with selecting, keeping, and raising Pomeranians. The publisher and the author think it is important to point out that the advice and information for Pomeranian maintenance applies to healthy, normally developed animals. Anyone who acquires an adult dog or one from an animal shelter must consider that the animal may have behavioral problems and may, for example, bite without any visible provocation. Anxiety-biters are dangerous for the owner as well as the general public.

Caution is further advised in the association of children with dogs, in meeting with other dogs, and in exercising the dog without a leash.

All inquiries should be addressed to:
Barron's Educational Series, Inc.
250 Wireless Boulevard
Hauppauge, NY 11788
http://www.barronseduc.com

International Standard Book No. 0-7641-1046-2

Library of Congress Catalog Card No. 99-43592

Library of Congress Cataloging-in-Publication Data
Stahlkuppe, Joe.
    Pomeranians : everything about purchase, care, nutrition, breeding, behavior, and training / Joe Stahlkuppe.
        p. cm. — (A Complete pet owner's manual)
        Includes bibliographical references (p.   ) and index.
        ISBN 0-7641-1046-2 (pbk.)
        1. Pomeranian dog. I. Title. II. Series.
SF429.P8S73   2000
636.76—dc21   99-43592
                                                       CIP

Printed in Hong Kong

9 8 7 6 5 4 3 2